Richard —

Keep chasing the 911 truth

Enjoy

Samuel E. Stein

THE NAKED TRUTH ABOUT DRUGS

daniel e. williams

CRONIN HOUSE

PUBLISHED BY CRONIN HOUSE

ISBN: 0-9760494-0
Copyright © 2004 by Daniel E. Williams
All Rights Reserved
Printed in the United States of America
2004
First Edition

for camel wellington and sweet melissa

Author's Preface

I was born in 1950. Growing up, when peer maturity passed me by as if I were standing still, Mom always said I was a late bloomer, imparting little comfort at the time. But being a late bloomer worked out surprisingly well in many aspects of my life, none more important than my association with drugs. I was fascinated by the counterculture in the 60s, especially the music, even though I didn't drink and wasn't in any hurry to try marijuana. When I finally did in 1970, it was on a fraternity house fire escape with a fellow ROTC cadet. Since that time I have done every drug on the menu. And I have learned two things: drugs are an adult pleasure and the government is deceiving us.

For nearly one hundred years our government has been wrong about drugs, about the people who use them and the risks they pose to society. Much of what they report is blatant misinformation, if not outright lies, despite a veneer of good intentions. It is also my contention millions of Americans agree with me. And it is not just the millions doing drugs responsibly, either. It is the millions more who've come to see society's approach to the drug crisis generate much more harm than good. They cut across all age, income and race demographics. Over the last thirty-plus years I've made it a point to talk with a number of them. And listen.

What I've gathered reflects not so much a change of mind as it does a change of heart. We still consider drugs to be harmful, but have come to view our drug laws as worse – and many of us no longer consider legalization a four-letter word. But when Richard Nixon first convened his drug war council, escalating the conflict, hardly anyone outside of what was derisively labeled the "lunatic fringe" favored legalization. How dare we, they scolded, when marijuana turned innocents into murderers and LSD would sufficiently scramble our DNA to produce three-headed babies. None of that was true of course, but it is what our government wanted citizens to believe. And many did.

But that was then. This is now. And it seems sadly ironic those who continue to support drug prohibition now occupy the lunatic fringe. For with the benefit of nearly four decades perspective, we see truth trumpeting government fiction: a pan of warm brownies and a quart of cold milk are the only things I've killed stoned, and three-headed babies are themselves hallucinations, existing only in supermarket tabloids. We have come to see the responsible use theory, the one so close to the alcohol lobby heart, parallel itself in the illicit drug environment: as not every drinker is a drunkard, so too is not every drug user an abuser.

The Naked Truth About Drugs explores America's affinity for drugs, providing historical context, and my own, on virtually every drug we consume. And some of what you will read may surprise you. All drugs were legal and cheap and readily available in America prior to 1914, and we were even encouraged to use them. Heroin was available from the Sears mail order catalog, as was morphine, opium and cocaine. But if you couldn't wait for the mailman, all those same drugs were sold at the corner grocery or drugstore. Our addiction rate then was very low, near identical to now. And we had no drug crime.

What changed it all, what disrupted our peaceful co-existence, was the Harrison Narcotics Act of 1914, a confluence of religious arrogance and racial bigotry, spread by a surprisingly small number of men and all tinged with political opportunism. All of which metastasized over the years and morphed into Richard Nixon's War on Drugs. Except now it was mostly white middle-class kids doing the drugs, questioning government authority by protesting our war with Vietnam. In turn, the government questioned their patriotism and gave raise to bumper-sticker politics, the most banal being "America: Love it or Leave it."

There are a variety of sound arguments for the repeal of drug prohibition. One is the Declaration of Independence, which guarantees our right to life, liberty and the pursuit of happiness, arguing the sovereignty of our bodies. Another is the Constitution, which defines treason against our United States as "levying war against them, or in adhering to their Enemies, giving them Aid and Comfort." We are not fighting drugs per se; we are levying war against those who use them. Drug prohibition has enriched our enemies with hundreds of billions of dollars and will guarantee hundreds of billions more, giving more than enough aid to any comfort. At least that's how the arguments go.

The best argument, where I believe we share the greatest commonality and the least polarity, is the one for law and order. The hugely inflated prices addicts pay for illegal drugs force many into a life of crime, committing nearly all our larceny-thefts, crimes the FBI report as non-violent. And though some addicts would just as soon shoot you as look at you, most drug violence occurs at the higher echelons of the black market, stemming from territorial and distribution conflicts. Repealing drug prohibition will bankrupt the black market and reduce the overall Crime Index by at least 50%, an argument central to the debate and hard to counter.

History is replete with drug stories and tales both good and bad, but all provide empirical data, unequivocal in its conclusion, that drugs are here to stay. So we are going to live with them one way or another. We lived in peace for over a century and have been at war nearly as long, ninety years. And rumor has it drug warriors, no longer intent on maintaining the status quo, have plans on paper just itching to be implemented that will end the drug war once and for all. It will not be pretty, making today's methods seem almost quaint. And we will all be doomed to failure, simply because we like drugs.

We drink, we smoke, we ingest and inject. It is part of who we are that no policy can change, no law. So we change our law and policy. But the biggest canard of the drug debate portrays those favoring repeal as being "soft on drugs." Not at all true. We're just being hard on stupidity. Which is why ending drug prohibition is society's smartest step toward jackhammering all those good intentions paving the way to hell.

THE NAKED TRUTH
ABOUT DRUGS

NAKED TRUTH I

Marijuana

It was the British who gave a young America her first
taste of marijuana, via extracts and elixirs known back then
as patent medicines: syrups designed to distract mankind
from the mundane and monotonous lives most led at the
time – and maybe do a little something for that toothache,
too. Concocted mostly from the *cannabis sativa* plant, with
THC being the only active ingredient in many, these medicines sold very well in America's frontier days. The problem wasn't that patent medicines were socially acceptable
to many – which they were – but that the many didn't know
what they were taking. Patent medicines were unregulated
and free from listing ingredients; everybody got high but
few knew why.

Those marijuana tinctures remained popular, but it
wasn't until 1876 before Americans realized you could
smoke it too. It happened that year at the World Exposition
held in Philadelphia to celebrate our Declaration of Inde-

pendence turning one hundred. It was a pretty big deal, to say the least. In honor of such an historic celebration, the Sultan of Turkey invited one and all over to his Pavilion to smoke a particular Turkish treat, and graciously hosted America's first pot party – and all in the name of freedom. Rumor has it smoke was so thick folks got high just walking by.

But it was the Industrial Age and most Americans were somewhat giddy anyway, so smoking marijuana seemed the perfect compliment. Turkish smoking parlors opened in larger northern cities to great success, drawing as much from the upper crust as any other. However, when the buzz wore off, so to speak, marijuana was just no match for alcohol, and all those smoking parlors went bust. That is, until certain folks with more time on their hands than common sense went about waging the crusade for teetotalism. Most of them were nuts, of course, but they squirreled around long enough to get Prohibition passed into law, fostering a resurgence in marijuana smoking.

Nowhere was that resurgence more evident than in New Orleans. A port city with a lively ethnic confluence, she became the natural birthplace of jazz – and a party lover's paradise. Marijuana was cheap in the Big Easy, and popular inside the mostly black jazz community of musicians and fans. And such a high time they must have had, witnessing the creation of a musical genre that still thrills the world. But there's always a little trouble in any paradise.

When a wave of violence rippled through New Orlean's black community, none other than newspaper tycoon – and textbook xenophobe – William Randolph Hearst trumped-up pot as the villain. Bold headlines in his tabloids labeled it the Marijuana Menace, and the stories, many personally penned by Hearst, were often race-baiting diatribes, Hearst's patented method of demonizing a practice in order to demonize the practitioner. Within a few years, in 1924, Louisiana and fourteen other states enacted laws criminalizing marijuana possession and its use. The law may have changed, but the complexion of users did not. Which made Mr. Hearst and his many minions, as one can imagine, feel very red white and blue.

But it was less bigotry and more hard-knuckle economics that precipitated the next change in marijuana's legal status. The Roaring Twenties ran us straight into the Great Depression, and we went from giddy to gloomy literally overnight. Most of America was out of work and standing long lines looking for it. Out west was no different. Except that menial jobs westerners once shunned were now coveted and the migrants holding them suspect – nothing like a little fear and loathing to light the nationalistic fuse.

To free-up jobs for our unemployed, different harassments were employed to persuade migrants of the wisdom in packing up and going home, including the 1931 law enforcing Mexican repatriation, a variant of the catch and release theory for fish, but for humans. While such shameful methods were generally effective, stragglers presented a nagging problem.

Drinking bootleg booze was the favored extracurricular activity for most westerners, and smoking marijuana did it for many migrants. It was a very clear distinction. And one that fit the bill for politicians keen to keep racist sentiments where they belonged – behind closed doors and just among friends, like Hearst. It had been awhile since Louisiana, and he smelled fresh blood in the water. With his encouragement, fictionalized stories of murder and mayhem in south of the border towns circulated about, and all attributed to Hearst's Marijuana Menace – with the strong inference it was heading our way. And there was no time to lose.

So to speed things up, four western states – Texas, California, Arizona and Colorado – aggressively petitioned the federal government to pass anti-marijuana legislation as a covert way to permanently pink-slip the migrants. They chose the newly established Federal Bureau of Narcotics (FBN) and its first Commissioner of Narcotics, Henry J. Anslinger, to do their dirty work.

But Anslinger had enough dirty work of his own, taking on the heroin and cocaine trade. He wasn't crazy about his new job, but did want to keep it. And trying to convince Congress to outlaw a weed that grew wild everywhere in the world except the Arctic Circle was not something the Commissioner viewed as a wise career move. So he tossed it back to the states.

They were not amused, nor, and more directly to the point, was William Randolph Hearst. Anslinger was invited or summoned – take your pick – to California and Hearst's San Simeon castle for a chat. The Commissioner was somewhat taken aback to find so powerful a man literally obsessed with marijuana, but sensed the issue just might be the golden hook to hang his hat. Now all he had to do was convince Congress and America unholy sex and murder lurked inside the minds of marijuana "addicts."

Anslinger's strategy was simple: scare every single parent in America clean out of their wits, as he was smart enough to know, federal law or not, enforcement would be next to impossible. So he focused on making propaganda films depicting how just one puff of the stuff would make you crazy enough to screw the cat and hack your mom to death with a meat cleaver. (If you think I'm exaggerating, then you haven't seen *Reefer Madness*. Considered the *piece de resistance* of marijuana propaganda films, *Reefer Madness*, released in 1936, tells the tale of a high school boy instantly transformed into a raving lunatic after a single puff of marijuana. He then becomes the pied piper of pot, leading other poor innocents to madness and even death.)

Anslinger succeeded in demonizing marijuana, but fell short of crafting a law to ban it that would pass constitutional scrutiny. He could not have been a happy man, what with Hearst and all those angry states festering like a boil on his backside. He suffered for nearly six years before relief finally arrived. The salve was contained in the Supreme Court decision concerning the National Firearms Act, a law aimed at controlling the proliferation of machine guns, the favored weapon used by Prohibition-era gangsters.

The National Firearms Act said it was illegal for anyone to give, borrow or trade away a machine gun without first having a Machine Gun Transfer Stamp. But the government flatly refused to make or issue such a stamp. Despite the clumsy logic, the Supreme Court ruled the law constitutional. Within hours, Anslinger broke out the party hats and cigars.

It wasn't very long before Anslinger had his own little stamp: the Marijuana Tax Stamp. Next the FBN drafted the Marijuana Tax Act, a virtual twin to the National Firearms Act, same clumsy logic and all: you had to provide pot to get that first stamp, but when you went to buy the stamp, pot in hand, you were busted for not having a stamp. Anslinger was then ready for his fifteen minutes and, with the Capitol Dome his Big Top, a circus disguised as congressional hearings began April 27, 1937.

And the only one not covered with grease paint was Doctor William Woodward, testifying on behalf of the American Medical Association. He refuted Anslinger's assertion marijuana use was near epidemic on school playgrounds, calmly stating the evidence just wasn't there. Period. But Congress, deaf in all ears after six years listening to Anslinger's hypnotic drumbeat, hooted and booted Woodward right out the rotunda door. In almost no time at all, on August 2, 1937, the Marijuana Tax Act was law. Anslinger and Hearst were working up a good head of steam.

And they used it to roll over the only other voice of reason challenging their position. Back in New York City, Mayor LaGuardia decided to form his own commission to study marijuana. Anslinger, in what can only be described as delusional arrogance, didn't object and even supplied the pot. But when his commission found marijuana to be of little harm and certainly no menace, LaGuardia found himself in political Siberia. And his only ticket home was on Anslinger's bus. LaGuardia got onboard. And that was that, folks.

Smoking marijuana went from being a toast of the town celebrating one hundred years of the Declaration of Independence to a declaration for war – in an historical blink and all on the hands of a bigot and a bureaucrat. It really is no more complicated than that. Prosecution of the new law was at times very selective, targeting popular actors and musicians, but always aggressive. Then World War II left us feeling our oats, or at least feeling we could trust our government. And we did. Maybe too much.

Hearst remained relentless until silenced by death in 1951, though his ghost still haunts. Anslinger soldiered on, spending nearly forty years fighting the Marijuana Menace, all of it as director of the Federal Bureau of Narcotics. He retired in 1967, undoubtedly proud of his accomplishments, only to receive as one parting gift a Supreme Court challenge to his beloved Marijuana Tax Act.

The Supreme Court of Lyndon Johnson's administration opted to hear the challenge. The Court's petitioners argued, simply, that the acquisition of a Marijuana Tax Stamp required self-incrimination, and therefore unconstitutional. The Supreme Court agreed, striking down the law. Anslinger was crushed. Salt in the wound was that Timothy Leary instigated the challenge. (Leary did have his moments.) Marijuana was in federal legal limbo when Richard M. Nixon took office.

Richard Nixon came to power on the promise of restoring law and order to a nation he believed was literally and metaphorically going to pot. And while a little paranoia can be a good thing, Nixon had it in spades and went absolutely apoplectic over marijuana (and Leary, calling him "the most dangerous man in America"). Passing a new federal anti-marijuana law became an obsession, resulting in the Comprehensive Drug Abuse Prevention and Control Act, neatly consolidating more than 50 pieces of existing drug legislation. Congress once again donned their clown suits, passing the Act in 1970.

Title II of Nixon's new Act, a provision known as the Controlled Substances Act, placed all drugs into five different categories, or schedules, according to their danger and potential for abuse. (And, in a bit of planned sleight of hand, effectively positioned the government between doctor and patient privilege in drug therapy decisions.) Armed with such a powerful law, and to show that he meant business, Nixon scheduled marijuana in the same category with heroin. And we were off to the races.

The depths of Nixon's marijuana paranoia cannot be overstated. His secret Oval Office recording system offers proof. In transcripts of conversations held during 1971 and 1972, and recently released by the National Archives, President Nixon can be heard advocating an "all-out war on all fronts" against marijuana smokers. Plus, he was absolutely convinced Jews and the Commies were behind it all. Nixon: "...every one of the bastards out for legalizing marijuana is Jewish. I suppose it's because most of them are psychiatrists." And "that's why the Communists and left-wingers are pushing this stuff." Marijuana arrests during that period skyrocketed to over 400,000 from 100,000.

Federal funding for all state and local drug war programs became a simple numbers game. The more marijuana arrests you made, the more federal monies you received. And marijuana busts were easy to make. Offenders were typically non-violent – mostly looking to kill nothing more than a bad case of munchies – thereby greatly reducing the risk to police officers. Which changed the dynamics of police work. Harder and more violent crime wasn't neglected, but a fixation on marijuana smokers became Job One. No one should believe otherwise. How else to explain that 400% increase in arrests between 1971 and 1972?

A fuller context includes the war in Vietnam. Part and parcel to the whole marijuana affair had Richard Nixon and Henry Kissinger doing their worst best to end the war with honor. Anti-war sentiment, Nixon fervently believed (as well as it all being a Commie pot plot), fundamentally weakened whatever position of strength his administration brought to those negotiations, and Kissinger just said Whatever it takes, Dick. That reality must not be discounted in any serious marijuana discussion, as demonizing a practice to demonize the practitioner was settled law.

Richard Nixon won re-election, decisively. And an unprecedented escalation of his drug war soon followed. Budgets ballooned. Boots hit the ground, running. Nixon had his game face on, and he wanted to win. But Watergate was the 800-pound gorilla sitting in the Oval Office when Nixon arrived for his second term, and it peeled him like a banana inside of 7 months. With his resignation just weeks away, Nixon, arguably not in the best of mental states, penned an Executive Order creating the Drug Enforcement Administration. To have wandered drunk around the White House talking to portraits of dead presidents, Richard Nixon can be forgiven. But not for the DEA.

Gerald Ford may have got his promotion with a promise for pardon, but he was an able caretaker for an America near comatose in the wake of Nixon's resignation. Not much really happened on his watch, save the collective deep sigh of relief we finally managed to take. But we still smoked pot. And law enforcement, habituated to federal drug money, continued marching on. The edge softened somewhat under Ford, and Jimmy Carter seemed to want marijuana decriminalized, but he was haunted by lust in his heart and a rabbit or two. Not to mention the failed rescue mission in Iran.

Ronald Reagan brought the hostages home and Morning to America when he reported to the White House stage. We loved the guy. His Star Wars was derided as fantasy, but the reality is it caused the Soviet Union to crater, then collapse. It was another Reagan fantasy, however, that failed to deliver: Just Say No. Nancy Reagan was an admirable advocate in all her efforts, but many millions of average and otherwise law-abiding Americans continued saying yes. And marijuana remained popular as a recreational pleasure throughout Ronald Reagan's two presidential terms.

Papa Bush rode Reagan's coattails to the White House, just as cocaine and its evil twin, crack, hit their peak. Greater powers had been given to the DEA, and by 1990 total drug arrests rose to 1,089,500, nearly double that of 1980. While marijuana was hardly ignored, cocaine remained the domestic focus of Bush, but his stiff upper lip on taxes quivered and cost him re-election, notwithstanding his qualified success in routing Saddam from Kuwait. And then Bill Clinton came to power.

Many hopes were raised that common sense would finally come to the drug debate. After all, he was the first baby-boomer president. But quicker than you can say "I didn't inhale," Clinton blew his considerable political capital, like some crazed drunk betting it all on one throw at a Vegas craps table, on "don't ask, don't tell" and socialized medicine. And left drug policy bromides to be issued by the diminutive doyenne heading his Department of Health and Human Services, Donna Shalala.

In what could have only caused Hearst's cold, dead heart to warm, Donna Shalala updated his Marijuana Menace in an op-ed page article published August 18, 1995 in the *Wall Street Journal*. And it should be required reading for anyone believing the mentality of our policy makers has changed a whit since *Reefer Madness*. But for those without the time or ready resources to look it up, allow me a Cliff's Notes-style treatment.

In a nutshell, Donna Shalala spilled a lot of ink denouncing legalization and declared marijuana – and I'm not kidding here – the absolute root of all evil. Not terrorism, money or some other social peccadillo. Marijuana. And she did so in pure Chicken Little fashion, citing "new" evidence supporting the addictiveness of marijuana and how legalization would only make matters worse, but all without the (unintended) humor displayed in *Reefer Madness*. And – again, I'm not kidding here – that nothing short of our national future was at stake.

Now I don't know what you think of the *Wall Street Journal,* or even if you think of it at all, but it just might be the best newspaper in America. A pretty conservative lot on most social issues – but so what. They're good. So giving Donna Shalala a large platform for her views was no real surprise. And I wasn't surprised (okay, maybe a little) eleven days later when the *Journal's* Letters to the Editor page published three responses, none kind to Shalala's apocalyptic views. Which begs the question...

Just what the hell was Bill Clinton thinking? As it turns out now, I know exactly what he was thinking, and which head did the thinking. But that didn't really bother me – or the economy, which seemed to be humming right along. What did make me want to slap the Boy from Hope was his complicity in the drug war. Despite his sop to the MTV generation, Bill Clinton's last year in office produced 734,497 marijuana arrests, well more than double those in 1990, with 646,042 being for simple possession. Thanks, Bill.

Before George W. Bush became president, he was the governor of Texas. And before that he was pretty much a drunk. While George has no qualms admitting he abused alcohol before coming to Jesus, when it comes to illegal drug use, his coy "maybe I did, maybe I didn't..." seems an invitation for one to guess. So I'm guessing he did. I'm guessing he smoked pot and snorted coke. And I'm guessing he liked them both. But what I *know* is that it doesn't matter.

What matters, pure and simple, is that George didn't get caught. And while he came to the party early and left late (his self-described "young and irresponsible" period ended around his 40th birthday), let's accept his claim that "what matters is how I behave as an adult," along with the implication drug use didn't impair his cognitive skills. But what's harder to accept is his advice to America: "If I were you, I wouldn't tell your kids that you smoked pot unless you want them to smoke pot. I think it's important for leaders and parents not to send mixed signals." Yeah, like how important it is to always tell the truth.

Hell may have no fury like a woman scorned, but a reformed druggie comes close. It wasn't enough George Bush advised parents lie to their children, he backed it up by arresting hundreds of thousands of them, insuring none would ever grow up to be president. In 2001, the first year of his presidency, total drug arrests were 1,586,902, with 723,628 being for marijuana, and 641,109 of those – nearly 90% – for simple possession. Read this short paragraph again. In the few seconds it takes, another hapless and harmless individual will be arrested in America for simple marijuana possession. Who's next?

Probably me. Again. July 11, 1971, in the summer of Nixon's discontent, I came butt to boot with one Murrill E. Johnson, a Columbus, Ohio policeman. Officer Johnson and his partner responded to a neighbor's complaint over the comings and goings and loud music at a party celebrating a friend's acceptance to medical school. When a lovely but very stoned girl answered the door, the thick smoke hit both cops in the kisser and the shit hit the fan.

The two policemen freaked and started blowing their whistles, shouting "nobody move" and "you're all under arrest." It was pandemonium and, in the true spirit of brotherhood, every man for himself. And every woman, too. People went flying out every door, every window and just about everywhere else. At least that's what my friends told me, as I was fast asleep in an upstairs bedroom. And that's about the time I got my not so gentle wake-up call from Murrill Johnson.

Pulled to my feet and handcuffed, I got the heave-ho down a flight of stairs, tumbling head over heels to the landing below. When I made it to the first floor, still shackled but fully awake, I knew the party was over. As did several others, also rudely awakened, standing cuffed together off to the side, feeling every bit as miserable as me. And Murrill E. Johnson got his man.

Or did he? Conviction rates didn't seem the priority then, just arrests. That's where the money was. There and defense lawyers. One of which my staunch Republican father hired (yes, things were quite tense). But the lawyer said not to worry, adding the comfort that comes in numbers, as the same thing was going on all over the country. And probable cause was a problem in most cases – and that mine was no different. He did find the circus-like atmosphere surrounding the arrest amusing, though.

As my lawyer predicted, probable cause was a problem, and when my case finally found its way to a courtroom, the judge threw it out. And with prejudice, which, in legal parlance, means it all never happened. But Murrill Johnson didn't see it that way. And it didn't help when folks in the courtroom snickered at my lawyer's suggestion the whole fiasco resembled a Keystone Kops episode. We would meet again, because they say everybody needs a hobby, and I became Murrill Johnson's.

Less than nine months later, around 3:45 in the morning, I was up against the wall and naked with the business end of a police revolver six inches from my left temple. And Murrill Johnson was in my right ear, almost at a whisper, gloating no hotshot lawyer would save me this time and giving graphic insights to my probable sex life in prison. My roommate was undergoing similar niceties in his bedroom. And the two young women with us were petrified.

My roommate and I were cuffed and herded into the front room, joining the girls. All of us were naked. It would be nearly an hour before the girls were allowed to cover up, time the police spent ogling and ransacking. We weren't allowed to go to the bathroom unaccompanied, and one girl just couldn't hold it. No stereo speaker or bookcase was left unturned. But there were no more drugs to be found. Only the ones poorly tossed in panic out my roommate's open window, a small pouch which dropped to the fire escape below, bouncing like a easy two-hopper to the policeman on his way up.

The girls would be released and not charged, something they were informed early on, which made the naked indignity of it all somehow bearable. We understood their not wanting to keep in touch. Besides, we were preoccupied. Being officially charged with "illegal possession of hallucinogens" and "keeping a house where hallucinogens are kept," we faced 2-10 years in prison. All for an ounce and a half of pot, several good hits of LSD and a few orange sopors: all the contents of that pouch we pitched to the police. Not exactly the contraband of a kingpin. But Murrill E. Johnson got his man, again.

And lost him, again. It seemed odd so many police cruisers would just converge in an alley, especially in the wee hours of the morning, but that was their story. And then there was the fire. "On April 23, 1972 about 3:45 a.m., I observed a fire in Apt. #5, of 1468 Michigan Ave., east side window" is a direct quote from officer Johnson's written statement. The reason they opened our front door with an ax, apparently. Once inside they found nothing burning, save a candle on the sill of that east side window, but Murrill Johnson swore he smelled smoke. Marijuana smoke. And, well, he just couldn't ignore that.

Well, the judge just couldn't ignore why so many of the city's finest had nothing better to do but hang out in a campus alley at 3:45 in the morning. Or why the fire department wasn't summoned. Not to mention the near-complete destruction of our apartment, which Murrill Johnson tried to justify, playing-off as mere coincidence it being mine. And then there was the matter of the naked girls. The judge found that very disturbing and downright rude. After a stern admonition to the state for their lewd and unlawful conduct, he dismissed the charges, again with prejudice, all of which visibly angered officer Johnson. I got the sense his hobby would become an obsession. Lucky me.

College started out pretty easy, though. And all I wanted to do was fly jets for the Air Force. I wore my blue ROTC uniform with pride for two years, passing the initial Air Force Officer Qualification Test and pilot/navigator physical. Walking the OSU campus three days a week in uniform, I developed a healthy skepticism for the "he ain't heavy, he's my brother" sentiment. I would incur many a dirty look and warmonger mumblings from my longhaired brethren. Flower girls were more passive, but their expressions said Never in a million years, buddy. It was all very interesting, to say the least.

I didn't get to fly fighters for the Air Force. And I never finished college, something my mother still hasn't forgiven. But I felt, quite literally, lucky to get out of town alive. Murrill Johnson may very well have been a good man, but he was a bad cop. And I was tired of being his hobby. My nerves were nearly shot. I had a hard time believing society hated me, although their Valentine wasn't very funny. But there was, as it seems with most dark clouds, a silver lining.

Things had gone beyond tense with my father, but when he realized just how badly the state wanted to ruin my life, and his by extension, much of the faith he lost in me shifted. He didn't start wearing love beads and listening to Dylan, or even think that I was right, but did come to believe the law wrong. And until it changed, he believed the sensible thing was not to smoke marijuana. But I believed, and still do, the only sensible thing was just the opposite. Because when good people obey bad law, bad law never changes.

And it is high time we change the law. Smoking pot poses no more threat to society than social drinking, if that. Yet it is the height of hypocrisy when our elected leaders gather in fashionable Washington D.C. parlors of the powerful and wring their collective hands over marijuana, all the while consuming, many to excess, *their* drug of choice. It is all about choice, and the freedom to make it.

Telling my marijuana trials and tribulations is not for sympathy or even cathartic effect, as neither is warranted, but only to give added context to those times. And to let you know mine was just one of over 400,000 like stories playing out across Nixon's America. Since those times, more than

15,000,000 American sons and daughters have joined our ranks.

Is that really what we want, in this land of the free and home to the brave?

NAKED TRUTH II

LSD

It was 1938 when scientist Albert Hofmann, working in a Swiss laboratory for Sandoz Pharmaceuticals and searching for a chemical blood stimulant, produced the twenty-fifth substance in a series of lysergic acid derivatives: lysergic acid diethylamide, which he abbreviated LSD-25.

No further mention of the substance is known for five years. Then, on April 16, 1943, Albert Hofmann accidentally absorbed a small amount (most probably through his fingertips) while in his lab. He recounts the experience as "an uninterrupted stream of fantastic pictures, extraordinary shapes with intense, kaleidoscope-like play of colors," and gave the world a scientist's first analysis of LSD.

Based on the premise lysergic acid diethylamide produced the effect, and with a scientist's curiosity, Hofmann decides to recreate the experience. Three days later he carefully calculates what he believes enough LSD to generate a similar effect: 250 micrograms, which he dilutes in a glass of water and drinks. Mildly put, 250 micrograms was a miscalculation. The first two hours were far more intense than his accidental experience and, fearing he might just be going insane, Hofmann asked an aide to summon a doctor.

Hofmann's vital signs registered normal, the only visible change being extremely dilated pupils, behind which all the real action was taking place. After the initial impact passed, as did his fright, Hofmann entered a comfort zone. Closing his eyes produced a kaleidoscope of "unprecedented colors and plays of shapes." And he marveled how "every acoustic perception," like the sound of a passing car, "became transformed into optical perceptions" with "consistent form and color." Literally, sound became visible.

When the effect wore off, Hofmann was completely exhausted and went to bed. The next morning he felt "a sensation of well-being and renewed life flowed through me." When he later walked through his garden, the sun shining after a spring rain, "everything glistened and sparkled in a fresh light." And "all my senses vibrated in a condition of highest sensitivity." His world seemed different, "newly created."

Significant to Hofmann was "I could remember the experience of LSD inebriation in every detail." This led to his conclusion that "the conscious recording function was not interrupted," even after experiencing a "profound breakdown of the normal world view." He was further surprised LSD produced "such a far-reaching, powerful state" without a trace of hangover. He felt great, mentally and physically. So he told a few pals.

Hofmann sent a detailed report to Professor Werner Stoll, head of the pharmaceutical department at Sandoz, and copied Ernst Rothlin, the director of the pharmacological department. Both men were astounded, as never before had any known substance displayed *any* such effect in fraction-of-milligram doses. It seemed almost unbelievable. So Rothlin, along with two colleagues, repeated Hofmann's experiment, only with a dose of just 80 micrograms. (Curious but cautious, those scientists.) Even at such a reduced level of LSD, the effect was deemed impressive and fantastic. "All doubts about the statements in my report," Hofmann would write, "were eliminated."

All that happened in 1943, let's not forget. Long before Timothy Leary and Peter Max and Ken Kesey's Merry Pranksters, before Tom Wolfe authored his *Electric Kool-Aid Acid Test* and the gonzo Hunter S. Thompson, before the Grateful Dead and Pink Floyd and *Sgt. Pepper's Lonely Hearts Club Band*. And before just about all else from the 60s and 70s we've come to associate with LSD.

But not long before the CIA, still looking for that perfect truth serum. They began testing LSD in the early 50s, but the unpredictable hallucinations of willing (and some unwitting) subjects during interrogation sessions provided more hindrance than help, yet presented a conundrum to the CIA. If it wasn't a reliable truth serum, could it be an effective lie serum? The thinking went if one of our spies fell to the enemy, swallowing a tiny LSD pellet would render the agent delusional and useless. Until the LSD wore off, that is. So by all accounts (but who *really* knows), it is believed CIA mind control experiments using LSD ceased by the decade's end.

The most promising research seemed to be in the field of mental health. Shortly after Albert Hofmann's intentional experiment that day in 1943, Doctor Werner Stoll pioneered LSD research on schizophrenics as well as healthy subjects, in doses ranging from just 20 micrograms to 130, conducted at the University of Zurich. His published results were inconclusive regarding therapeutic application, but he pointedly cited the high activity of LSD as indicative of potential use as a research tool for psychiatry.

After that little icebreaker in Zurich, it was cosmic-conscious Katie bar the door. A fair number of psychotherapists and psychiatrists began testing LSD on patients, with notable successes. And they took it too. Dr. Stoll, in those same published results, recounted his experience of taking 60 micrograms of LSD. His LSD inebriation was of less magnitude than Hofmann's, yet there were similarities in anxiety and euphoria. So those who spoke most knowingly about LSD were the early practitioners. Those who denounced it were primarily non-practitioners, the ignorant. Which is the crux of the LSD biscuit.

Think of LSD as brain surgery. Would you want the surgery performed by some guy who watched it on the Discovery Channel, or would you want a real brain surgeon? Exactly. And as such, who better to believe about LSD than those pioneers leading the way? So forget for a moment all the non-practitioner guesswork, all the propaganda from all governments, all the media hype, all the blue-ribbon panels, and just think about having that brain surgery.

Okay, that's enough. Now let's talk about me. Albert Hofmann beat me to the punch by twenty-seven years. It was the summer of 1970, not long after my first joint out on the fire escape, when I first took LSD. It was Orange Sunshine and that experience will remain, until the day I die and get to see it all, the most enlightening of my life. Period. And thank you very much, Albert.

A girl I'll call Alice was someone I met in high school, different, and we hit it off. Romance was in the air for a short period, but we worked better as friends. And after high school we went away to different colleges, staying loosely in touch. Alice called me that mid-summer day and, with great enthusiasm, asked if I had taken LSD. I said I had not, so she asked if I was interested. I was. Plans were made.

We met in the early morning several days later and headed for John Byron State Park, a beautiful and favorite spot not far from home. On the way, Alice described LSD as, um, indescribable, but knew I would like it. All I really needed to do was keep an open mind, she said, enjoy and not be afraid. Said it would change my world. Alice was a smart and sensible young woman and I trusted her judgment. We made it to John Byron and took the LSD.

Albert Hofmann's first deliberate tripping the light fantastic had nothing on mine. When the LSD came on, all that I thought I knew, all that I considered real, all of just about everything, changed. I can't say I went out of my mind; the borders being debatable, but going out of body is quite the surreal event. And the wild and vivid hallucinations were an absolute joy to behold, many presenting unmitigated rapture. I still get goose bumps.

At first they came in constant waves, one spectacular vision after another. With every hallucination came astonishment. Time seemed no longer a concept. The world was a swirling mirror, and every different sound was different. Soon a certain ebb and flow developed, the time between filled with excited conversation and hilarity. And of all the countless hallucinations that day, one clearly stands out as perhaps the finest.

As we tripped about in Mother Nature's splendor, and our own, my attention fixated on a white patch of puffball dandelions. I picked one and blew on it. The white puffs scattered, then instantly morphed into the most beautiful butterfly I'd ever seen. It was not some gauzy image, but fully formed and as absolutely real as you. And then it flew away. For what seemed an indeterminable length of time, but in all probability just seconds, I watched as it disappeared in very blue sky.

Nearly everything else remains in my mind's eye, most as close as thirty-three years ago. My moustache danced some kind of crazy jitterbug on my upper lip. Tickled me to death. I never lost knowing Alice, even when I would look and she wouldn't be her. What she was wasn't bad, and could talk. *That* was something else. Other times we seemed in telepathic connection. We'd nod and just smile. And then laugh til it hurt.

As the day wore on and the LSD began to taper off, and all too soon we agreed, hallucinations gave way to lovely visual trails quite like those from waving sparklers on the Fourth of July. Small birds flying overhead streamed tail feathers long and slender as a whip. The landscape seemed to have a pulse all its own. There was a sense of bounce to sunshine. The entire day was simply stunning. And then it was over.

LSD will wear you out. A morning trip guarantees an early night. However, the next day I felt like a million bucks. No hangover whatsoever and no residual visual effect. But I had changed and knew my world had as well. It did boggle the mind. How could such an amazing experience result from swallowing a little orange barrel hardly larger than my Zippo flint? I thought long and hard about the old adage man uses just 10% of the brain. And how maybe, just maybe, LSD bridged the remaining 90%.

So I couldn't wait to trip again. Over the next two years I took my fair share – and probably yours – in a wide variety of safe settings, enjoying best the outdoors. All were exceptional. There was a time at a friend's house when, just as Hofmann wrote, sound became visible. I don't remember the music we had playing, but it was blasting when three-dimensional musical notes, big ones and little ones and all in different colors, flowed from the room's cast iron radiator. Those were the days.

And throughout the three decades since, I've managed to keep my hand in. There have been periods of years between doing any hallucinogens, of any variety. And it wasn't any big deal. After those first two years of tripping at the drop of a hat, often at microgram doses exceeding Hofmann's, it became less an issue of just how much LSD I could do and more of just how much was needed.

Which was a core issue for those in the field of mental health. It worked for some patients but not nearly for all, no matter how often administered, leading critics to assume a certain "I told you so" posture. The other side argued LSD was just a tool, albeit a very good one, and not a panacea. Such esoteric debates had an element of navel picking, but by and large went looking for the truth, and not a truth serum.

Which, remember, was the CIA's game. We're still in the early 50s, and spies like us all over the world looked to LSD for deliverance. And they didn't get it. No surprise there, as LSD functions to unlock the mind – not control it. But when unwitting LSD subject Frank Olson committed suicide days after being given the substance, the CIA panicked, officially declaring the drug of no value. And later played a supporting role in determining its illegal status shortly after Timothy Leary spilled the beans.

Timothy Leary was a Harvard University professor. As a part of his research studying prison inmates, Leary gave them psilocybin, a natural hallucinogen found in certain mushrooms. He took it as well. It had positive effects on both. Preferring the "naturalness" of psilocybin, Leary resisted taking LSD at first. But when he did, it was Harvard colleague Richard Alpert's claim Leary remained mute for days, and was feared "lost." However, again according to Alpert, the first word Leary finally spoke was "Wow!" Interest in the recreational use soon followed.

Illustrative to such interest is the reverse chronology aspect, being early practitioners included more than a few on the cusp of middle age; respected doctors, artists of all stripes and academia. Demographic profiles fast-tracked to youth, yet the origins of LSD use remain central to the debate. Albert Hofmann and other very early LSD enthusiasts were hardly the anti-establishment radical types. They were sober, reasoned men.

And those who followed were not all that different, though the context of use shifted from the mentally ill to the mentally well. But it was Leary's message of "turn on, tune in and drop out" that radicalized the LSD debate (causing him untold miseries, many self-inflicted). Upwards of three million people took LSD in a relatively short period of time, with the overwhelming majority quite receptive to the experience. In any statistical sample this large, and any statistician will agree, such consensus cannot be dismissed.

But it can be feared. The early 50s commingled quiet scientific research with even quieter CIA research, while the decade's end brought the beginning of recreational use.

Harvard University and Leary established the Psychedelic Research Center in 1960, leading the FDA in 1962 to designate LSD an experimental drug, thus greatly restricting research. So research more or less moved to the street, in 1963, the same year Harvard fired Timothy Leary and Richard Alpert. Leary opened the League of Spiritual Development, citing LSD as its sacrament, in 1966, the same year California banned LSD. Which spawned the Summer of Love in San Francisco, in 1967, the same year LSD is banned federally. If this were all a game of chess, that last government move was check.

As mentioned previously, the Comprehensive Drug Abuse Prevention and Control Act passed in 1970. It was Title II of that legislation, dubbed the Controlled Substance Act, which placed drugs into categories according to their danger and potential for abuse, Schedule I being reserved for the worst. LSD and all hallucinogens were placed on Schedule I, right up front with heroin and marijuana. Checkmate. The game lasted barely 10 years.

So, what *really* happened? Let's examine the contemporary view. On an average day in a Swiss lab an above average scientist created LSD-25, a substance considered of little research value and ignored for five years, until 1943. Through accident, then deliberately, Albert Hofmann experiences LSD. And came to believe LSD, with proper preparation and administered under strict supervision, could prove valuable to those treating mental disorders. His theory was tested. Results were mixed but encouraging. Research continues. The CIA joins the bandwagon. Things get weird.

Timothy Leary grabs the microphone, and things get weirder. Almost three million people take LSD. Horror stories, real and otherwise, did not discourage use, as many would enthusiastically take it again. The media went shamefully wild, fueling the fire. And our government wanted desperately to put it out. Laws were passed by reasonable men and women, but in the true heat of the moment. All of which produced great generational discontent, manifesting as deep distrust in government. The government fought back. Leary is arrested in 1966, getting ten years for marijuana possession. He escapes in 1970 and is branded "the most dangerous man in America" by Nixon. And it's been the weirdest thing ever since.

I label all the above as the contemporary view, as it encompasses most everything everyone knows, and some only peripherally, about the history of LSD. But the knowledge and use of hallucinogens is many centuries old. So now is as good a time as any to buckle-up and bring God into the debate. To do so, we must travel back over three thousand years to Greek antiquity, to 1500 B.C., to The Mysteries of Eleusis.

Reality being whatever it is, one notion, the cleft reality experience (cleft meaning cleave or split), summarizes fairly as Man against the natural world. And has to a large extent shaped what has become our industrial/technical existence, putting us all in similar predicament. That predicament is the conscience we suffer for advancement extracted with improper balance from nature. It's like a mosquito on the ego. We're not always sure when it bites, but it always makes us itchy.

Attempts to correct that conflict began in Greek antiquity, with the grafting of the Dionysian worldview to that of the cleft reality experience. Derived from the Greek god Dionysus, it presented an ecstatic, more intuitive worldview as an attempt to obliterate that cleft. Those old Greeks loved

their gods, immortalizing them in drama, and great ceremonial festivals were held in honor of Dionysus. And these
festivals were connected, not the least spiritually, with The
Mysteries of Eleusis.

Their celebration of Demeter, wife of Zeus and goddess
of agriculture, provides pertinent prelude to The Mysteries.
Hades, god of the underworld, kidnaps Persephone, daughter of Zeus and Demeter, and refuses to give her back. In
retaliation, Demeter leaves Olympus and vows never to return, and lays fallow the earth, allowing nothing to grow
until Persephone is returned – the season us mortals now
refer to as winter.

Persephone broke bread with Hades, a most forbidden
act, and Zeus was not at all amused. But nothing was growing, either. Zeus found Demeter living in anonymous refuge among the mortals of Eleusis and offered her a deal.
Demeter could have her daughter back, but for just half of
each year. Persephone, as punishment for her grave indis-
cretion, would spend the other half with Hades. Demeter,
to mitigate the grief of absence, demanded the earth return
fallow during Persephone's banishment. Done.

But before leaving Eleusis, and to thank the good people
living there, Demeter identifies herself and founds a sacred
temple. It is there, in the inner sanctum, where she reveals secret teachings to an Eleusinian high priest named
Triptolemus, the first initiate into what came to be called
The Mysteries of Eleusis. A further gift was grain seed and
knowledge for its cultivation, which then spread throughout
the mortal world.

Told through the life cycle of Persephone, and tied to
the agricultural rhythms of Nature, the story of Demeter
was enacted in the fall of every year, in Athens, beginning

around 1500 B.C. Though of great overall significance to antiquity, the drama of Demeter forms but the outer construct of The Mysteries.

From Athens there was a religious procession of large numbers to Eleusis, a journey of roughly fifteen miles. Festivals and ceremonies filled their next two days, with specific rituals performed by that year's initiates, numbering as many as three thousand. All Greek-speaking persons, with murderers the sole exception, could present themselves as a potential initiate, but only once.

And many did. Aristotle, Plato and Cicero are among some of the more prominent initiates, yet it was a common man experience as well – and an honor for all. But every initiate took a life oath never to speak directly of what each experienced inside the inner sanctum, not that such an intensely personal revelation could be adequately expressed.

Archeological artifacts from that time draw a good picture of these events, but not much is known of actual inner sanctum activities: the oath of silence was strictly observed. Though all initiates were forbidden to speak *of* the experience, many spoke *to* it, and in language unmistakable as to the visionary nature of the revelations. Which is a nice corollary to the hallucinogenic experience in modern times.

Widely accepted by Eleusinian scholars is the theory a liquid potion was consumed by each initiate – the final ritual inside the inner sanctum. This potion, prepared by learned herbalists, was called *kykeon,* and contained barley extract and mint as two ingredients. And was most certainly hallucinogenic in nature, giving corroboration to the ecstatic resonance which infused all spoken *to* accounts. A very good question, though, is just where did those herbalists find such a potent ingredient?

Basically, it was growing all around them. Type "ergot of rye" into any Internet search engine and load your printer. The gist of it all, however, is ergot alkaloids act in similar fashion to lysergic acid diethylamide, and ergot, a kind of purple/brown fungi, grew on grains and grasses common to the fields surrounding Eleusis. (Albert Hofmann, in collaborating with Gordon Wasson and Carl Ruck on the 1976 book *The Road To Eleusis: Unveiling the Secret of The Mysteries,* presents fine argument for this ancient agricultural reality.)

So let's accept the premise that hallucinogens were taken by those initiated into The Mysteries of Eleusis. And that it was a good thing. After all, it did go on for nearly two thousand years, voluntarily too. Sounds to me there must have been something good going on. So why did they stop? Another very good question. And that's where God comes into the picture.

It was around 400 A.D. when another historical brute, the Gothic King Alarich, invades northern Greece and destroys Demeter's sacred temple, signaling demise for our ancient world. This demise was in no small measure hastened by the monks traveling with Alarich, spreading Christianity in the wake of conquest. And it wasn't long before Ecclesiastical Christianity, with its Creator/creation perspective, began its reign and rule over the interpretation of God.

This interpretation, the antithesis of the Dionysian and Eleusinian worldview, is the bedrock of Christianity, Judaism and Islam, the three main monotheistic religions of today. Whatever good can be said of organized religion, it cannot be left unsaid that much early conversion was merely coercion through wars, wars killing more in the name of God than any other. And that bell is still ringing.

The Mysteries of Eleusis fostered the interpretation of God not as a single, separate entity, but resident in all things, including the self. And it was in that inner sanctum, under the influence of ergot, where initiates experienced self the most. But denigrated as pagan ritual and blasphemy by Alarich and his monks, The Mysteries, after nearly twenty centuries of celebration by several million joyous initiates, ended.

So there you have it. Two diametrically opposite interpretations of God. But which one gets the Oscar? Is it the Creator/creation concept espoused by the world's three major organized religions? Or is it the one revealed through a cup of *kykeon* or a couple hundred micrograms of LSD? Well, from here in the cheap seats, organized religion is oxymoronic and God is simply Truth. And LSD provides a portal to Truth unmatched by any organized religion prognostication or parable of the last three millennia.

I told you to buckle-up. Now let's talk about another kind of flashback. The kind most certainly to be depicted had the movie *LSD Madness* ever been made. People who took LSD were expressly warned against "acid flashbacks," which could occur *at any time* in the aftermath of the experience. And we were told it wouldn't be pretty. Well, I'm going on record right now as saying I've never once experienced a flashback and, if I do say so myself, if anyone deserves a freebie, it's me. I feel cheated.

And even as I have never experienced a bad LSD experience, I'm quite aware others have. The real tragedy is many could have been avoided, as preparation is the key. Which speaks directly to the theory of set and setting in the taking of LSD. "Set" being where your head's at, with "setting" being your physical location. And paying a little attention to that theory, which most of the bad trippers did not, goes a long way.

Albert Hofmann lamented the fact his creation was used irresponsibly, and I agree. Though the potential for spontaneous ecstatic epiphany resides within us all, LSD is not for everyone. It is a very powerful substance, capable of animating in a most visceral way our deepest psyche, warts and all. And that alone is reason enough for many to avoid its use, as a dredging-up of the subconscious poses a frightening risk. But a sober understanding of such potent self-revelation can help navigate the ride.

And the ride should be taken among pleasant company, in comfortable surroundings. Most every hallucinogenic experience of mine was a (small) group effort, and those among the group not partaking watched over those who were. You certainly didn't want to babble on around strangers. They really don't care and, worse yet, may call someone you will most assuredly not want to meet. Set and setting. It works.

Meditation will not produce hallucinations, yet it is worth special mention here. Meditation has somewhat of a faddish history, at least in modern times. But for many, especially those long-term practitioners, it can nudge the mind across the everyday boundaries of life, enhancing its quality. It's really just a mental exercise, but it takes practice. Which is why, in our quest for instant gratification, it still gets the raised eyebrow of skepticism.

But I like it. It helped me not break a nail out there on the ledge awaiting my fate back in 1972. I was in Fort Lauderdale, where I began every day down on the beach, meditating as the sun rose in the east. It wasn't duck to water, but after six months I began to think I was on to something.

I still do. And over the past thirty-three years, hardly a day goes by where I don't go away for a while. It can be for twenty minutes or an hour. The length of time has come to be of minimal significance. Consistency is the key.

Albert Hofmann has led a very interesting life. As one of the 20th century's preeminent medical scientists, he stands out as the only one alive today with three medicines still in worldwide use. While such accomplishments place him in the medical Hall of Fame, his creation of LSD-25, and his subsequent notoriety, unfairly overshadow those contributions. At 98, he now lives quietly in Switzerland with his lovely wife.

As the creator of LSD-25, Albert Hofmann stood at the forefront of its history and knows the subject well – something we recently discussed in the cozy living room of his Swiss home. We drank homemade plum schnapps, told a few lies and solved the problems of the world. It was a wonderful afternoon. And while he credits genetics as important to his longevity, he is quick to add LSD as a contributor.

Many of Albert Hofmann's quotes in this section come from *LSD: My Problem Child,* a book he wrote in 1979, providing the reader an excellent perspective of the thirty-six years post-discovery. Though the title's parental tone reflects Hofmann's certain sadness LSD was misunderstood and misused, his enthusiasm has not diminished.

And *LSD: My Problem Child* should be read. It is an important and thoughtful work. But it's hard to find. The hardback had just one edition. Paperbacks are easier, but scarce nonetheless. So, chances are, not many will have the opportunity. But if you like your picture bigger, it's worth the search.

Albert Hofmann, on that unforgettable day we spent together, granted me permission to use his words in my book. And for that I am grateful beyond description. As such, I'd like to end with another direct quote. It is the final paragraph of *My Problem Child*. The italics are all Albert's.

I see the true importance of LSD in the possibility of providing material aid to meditation aimed at the mystical experience of a deeper, comprehensive reality. Such a use accords entirely with the essence and working character of LSD as a sacred drug.

Think brain surgery.

NAKED TRUTH IIa
Mescaline

Many like to dismiss as myth the use of *kykeon* in Greek antiquity, believing whatever archeological evidence exists as unreliable. Fair enough. But no one can dismiss the irrefutable data proving the peyote cactus, species *Lophophora williamsii,* a known hallucinogen, played an important role in the religious ceremonies of ancient Aztecs and Native Americans. Peyote buttons. They've been found strung around the neck of skeletal remains in Mexican burial caves, some considered 1,000 years old. While some Aztecs considered peyote God, all users believed it an agent for communing with God.

That, of course, did not sit well with the invading Catholic Spaniards. Immediately they set about to eliminate all forms of indigenous worship, setting the tone by destroying religious sites and records. Resistance of any kind was met with the kind of brutality and torture best left to the imagination. Still, the use of peyote continued, clandestinely. It was around Civil War time when American Indian tribes learned of the peyote ritual, and possibly of Aztec atrocities, adding a pinch of Jesus for good measure.

Just as our Native Indians were getting the hang of it, we were stoking the imagination of those who would chronicle just how the West was won. And they said we won a lot of it from the natives. It wasn't very pretty, as most of history and Hollywood suggests, or the emergence of the Ghost Dance any coincidence. Performed as a peyote ritual, the belief was that, if one's soul were pure and full of prayer, God would send down their ancestors and help destroy the white man, or at least bring him to his senses. It didn't work. And you can bet that little ditty *Home on the Range,* where seldom a discouraging word is heard, doesn't get much airplay on the reservations.

With little else to cling to, Native Americans fought for their right to consume peyote as a religious ritual. It took a while, but in 1918 the Native American Church was founded, permitting members to ingest peyote in religious ceremonies. Christians took a dim view, and over the next four decades numerous bills came before Congress seeking to ban the religious use of peyote. Now, can you imagine telling the Pope everything would be fine if Catholics just quit eating Jesus, symbolized in that little white wafer we eat? Me either. Yet it wasn't until 1960 when an Arizona judge ruled the religious use of peyote protected by the First and Fourteenth Amendments.

Stepping back to the 1880s, scientific studies of peyote led pharmaceutical companies to produce and distribute dried peyote buttons, minus the necklace, for the treatment of numerous mental disorders, as well as alcoholism. But no one actually knew what it was about peyote that caused its effect, encouraging science to get to the bottom of it all. Which occurred in 1897 when German chemist Arthur Heffter isolated peyote's active ingredient, naming it mescaline, no doubt a nod to an ancient oracle, the mescal bean. Mescaline was first synthesized in 1919, and various studies were conducted, including the extensive *Der Meskalinrausch,* published in 1927, in Berlin.

The first English language monograph postulating the therapeutic benefit of mescaline was published the following year, in 1928, written by American psychologist Heinrich Kluver. Titled *Mescal,* Kluver's work is a treasure trove of clinical data close to empirical in nature, detailing how mescaline provided psychologists a potent research tool for better understanding the depth and dynamics of human consciousness. What Kluver failed to address, perhaps in a desire to keep things neat, was the ancient custom tying mescaline to God, something of which he was undoubtedly aware.

Englishman Aldous Huxley attempted that exploration in his provocative book, *The Doors of Perception,* published in 1954. I say attempted only because *Doors* minimized the dogma of organized religion, examining instead how mescaline facilitated better understanding of the world around us. But in his next book, *Heaven and Hell,* published two years later, Huxley ventures into God territory, suggesting hallucinogens may help illuminate that path as well – the Bible's burning bush, revisited. We said he was crazy.

Albert Hofmann, long before creating LSD, was an admirer of Huxley, thinking him a great writer and thinker. Huxley's *Point Counter Point, After Many a Summer, Eye-*

less in Gaza and other works inspired him. But it was *The Doors of Perception* and *Heaven and Hell* that gave Hofmann a deeper insight into his own LSD experiments. The two men met first in 1961, at a Zurich hotel. Over lunch with their wives, conversations centered on the potential of hallucinogens, and the problems.

The irresponsible use of LSD had yet to materialize, but Albert Hofmann believed experimentation was best conducted under laboratory settings, something Huxley found to be insignificant, even counterproductive. Huxley contended such sterile environments inhibited the full potential of hallucinogens, suggesting, to make his point, Mrs. Hofmann take LSD in an alpine meadow and behold the wonder of creation by simply gazing into the blue cup of a gentian flower. Who knows, but the Hofmann's backyard meadows go on forever, and are beautiful. And at 94, so is Mrs. Hofmann.

Hofmann and Huxley met again during late summer of 1963, in Stockholm this time, attending the annual World Academy of Arts and Sciences convention. WAAS provided a forum where thoughtful and learned folks could take their shot at solving the problems of the world, free of ideological and religious constraints. Which, of course, meant most reports and publications printed were summarily dismissed, none quicker than Huxley's, advancing the thought Western culture could embrace hallucinogens as a means of augmenting for the better our reality experience – ala Dionysus but no Jesus.

Aldous Huxley and Albert Hofmann, writer and scientist, explored the deeper regions of the conscious mind, with tacit understanding the journey to be much of the destination, leaving breadcrumbs but no siren calls along the way.

This quiet exploration for man's hidden talent, even if it were not fully revealed, both believed would be of evolutionary significance, the next big step. We said they were crazy.

Sadly, that summer in Stockholm was the last they would be together. Huxley had advanced throat cancer, and would not live out the year. On his deathbed, convulsing and choking and no longer able to speak, Huxley wrote his wife a short note, instructions for what he knew was his last day. It read: "LSD--try it--intramuscular--100mmg." Laura Huxley, with love and all hope, injected her husband with LSD, providing him a serene and peaceful passing. To be among Huxley's last thoughts humbled Hofmann, as did a copy of his last words, given to him by Mrs. Huxley as a measure of unspoken gratitude.

Mescaline enjoyed only a brief run on the beatnik and counterculture stage, being quickly eclipsed by LSD. But as luck would have it, my next hallucinogenic experience that summer of 1970 came from mescaline. My dearly departed friend Bob bought it and we did it together, spending much of our day outdoors. Trees didn't speak to me this time, but they did wave. We were a far cry from Huxley and Hofmann, to be sure, but it's what I think about most when I think about Bob. It was such a beautiful day.

Aldous Huxley is best remembered for his novel *Brave New World,* written over just four months in 1931. Important to note, though a drug for the masses called *soma* figures prominently in the book, Huxley wrote *Brave New World* long before experiencing mescaline. *Soma* was designed to keep everyone comfortably numb, pseudo-freedom in a brutally efficient society fully controlled by an insane government. It was all pleasure and no pain, which Huxley believed was no pleasure at all.

Island, the flipside to *Brave New World,* appeared thirty-one years later, in 1962. Here Huxley employs another drug, which some believe to be idealized LSD, but one that celebrates and preserves the uniqueness of the individual, so essential to collective freedoms and sanity, two characteristics Huxley believed at great risk in our modern world. Say what you want about Huxley, but if you haven't read his work, say it softly. He was a man of intense curiosity and passion, and passed away November 22, 1963.

Camelot suffered doubly that day.

NAKED TRUTH IIb
Psilocybin

"There is a world beyond ours, a world that is far away, nearby, and invisible. And there is where God lives, where the dead live, the spirits and the saints, a world where everything has already happened and everything is known."

Sounds very much like something you might encounter reading the Bible, describing the heavenly attributes of afterlife, doesn't it? It does to me. Except it's not, at least not in the Biblical sense. These are the words of the famed Mazatec shaman, Maria Sabina, as relating to the world sacred mushrooms take her. It is a world that speaks a language of its own, one Sabina was known to understand and consult, seeking answers for those around her asking questions. All of which, at least, is according to R. Gordon Wasson.

Mr. Wasson was a New York City banker, vice-president of J.P. Morgan Company. Married to a pediatrician, both wrote *Mushrooms, Russia and History,* considered the standard reference on ethno-mycology, or the human use of fungi, specific, in this case, to hallucinogenic mushrooms. It is a two-volume work, published in 1957, two years after Maria Sabina spoke those words to Wasson, right before giving him access to the sacred mushrooms, becoming the first white man accorded such privilege.

Gordon Wasson and Albert Hofmann began a friendship shortly after Dr. Hofmann in 1958 first isolated, inside his Sandoz laboratory, the active ingredient in hallucinogenic mushrooms, naming it psilocybin. Invited by the Wassons in the fall of 1962 to join an expedition back to Mexico in search for another magic plant, *ska Maria Pastora,* or the "leaves of the shepherdess," used among the Mazatec in medicinal and religious ceremonies, the Hofmanns eagerly accepted. Another goal was finding Maria Sabina, in the hopes of sharing with her Hofmann's laboratory psilocybin, seeking her opinion as to how it compared to mushrooms in the raw.

It wasn't too long a strange trip, and, after a time, they obtained the shepherdess' leaves, but not an invitation to join in their ceremonial use, something the Mazatec held sacred and proprietary. But a healing priest, or *curandera,* convinced by Wasson or possibly through premonition that all could be trusted, agreed to conduct a ceremony, albeit in great secrecy. Crushing the leaves and creating a bitter potion, the *curandera* gave each a drink and performed her traditional rituals, confirming *ska Maria Pastora* held mushroom status as a sacred drug. Now, if they could just locate Maria Sabina.

And they did. Though Hofmann believed his synthetic psilocybin pills every bit the equal to sacred mushrooms, a confirmation from Maria Sabina would be nice. In a ceremony shrouded in similar secrecy and the same implied trust, Maria Sabina, the Wassons and the Hofmanns and several others traded one world for another with that other language, an experience Sabina deemed equal to the mushroom. Quite pleased but not surprised, Hofmann, upon leaving the next day, presented a vial of psilocybin pills to Sabina, who accepted them graciously and, being the *curandera* she was, humbly.

There exists debate as to whether Maria Sabina's introduction of the white man to sacred Mexican traditions was a blasphemy or a blessing. Both sides have merit. Yes, in all likelihood it is true without such risky exposure ancient customs would disappear, and really without a trace. And enough data published ensures perpetuity. But ignorance seems to shadow enlightenment, as publication led to an invasion by hippies and other drug seekers. Not everyone was nice, and some should be ashamed.

The use of hallucinogens as religious sacrament is a long established practice, one that will persist whether we like it or not. It provides an alternative to organized religion, while at the same time supplying much the same succor. And for those so inclined, it should not be banned, even though considered blasphemy – something we witness every Sunday in our less scrupulous TV evangelists. Praise the Lord and pay the piper.

While the discussion of hallucinogens in a sectarian context makes many a Christian uncomfortable, a discussion of their use in the secular context of behavior modification may provide more common ground or, at least, less emotion.

Just as Wasson and Huxley were making their way around Mexico, Dr. Timothy Leary was exploring the use of psilocybin as a therapeutic treatment among Massachusetts' maximum-security inmates in his Concord Prison Psilocybin Rehabilitation Project. His basic premise being psilocybin could reduce recidivism rates, or the number of ex-cons returning to prison. And remember, this was before anyone thought he was crazy.

Conducted during 1961 and 1962, with the support of Harvard University and willing assistance from the Massachusetts Correctional Institute, the project involved 32 inmates, Dr. Leary and a small but dedicated staff. The genesis of Leary's premise arose out of his preliminary research into the subjective effects of psilocybin, finding nearly 90% of subjects learned something of value about themselves and the world, while over 60% claimed psilocybin improved their daily lives. As such, Leary speculated psilocybin experiences might provide necessary catalysts for like behavioral modification in prisoners, enhancing the chance, once paroled, fewer would return to a life of crime.

And it was a noble undertaking. I sure wouldn't want to take psilocybin with prisoners, especially inside a prison, would you? So let's eliminate immediately any bias that Concord mirrored the Merry Pranksters. And, as quickly, acknowledge things didn't turn out exactly as Leary wanted us to believe. But everyone was diligent and worked hard on one of the toughest nuts society has yet to crack, the rehabilitation of the criminal mind. Treatment began with a variety of personality tests and four preparatory sessions, all of which were discussed in group therapy consisting of four inmates and two team members.

Then came the first psilocybin session, a daylong affair where inmates, guided by team members, freely discussed whatever entered their minds or, more precisely, flowed from them. Next, several group sessions were devoted to analysis and integration of the experience, as well as preparation for the second, and last, psilocybin treatment. As a show of committed support, one team member also took psilocybin, while the other documented events. After the final experiment, that same battery of personality tests was again administered, again with feedback to participants.

Leary and his team were confident of success, and seemed convinced by the results from the initial follow-up, conducted a mean 18 months after subject testing, reporting a recidivism rate of just 32% against the 56% found among all 311 inmates discharged or paroled from Concord in 1959. Additionally, slapping a little icing on his psilocybin cake, Leary claimed most of that 32% returned to prison for technical violations of parole, not new crimes. And that's when things got a little dicey, on a couple of levels.

It now appears, thanks to extensive research by Rick Doblin and his Multidisciplinary Association for Psychedelic Studies (MAPS), and through confirmation by Dr. Ralph Metzner, an original team member, the long-term effect of psilocybin on recidivism was negligible. Not only that, but Leary's initial 32% recidivism rate seems to have been, either intentionally or by error, incorrect. And the number of inmates returned for mere parole violation, Leary's icing, seems massaged. Which is all such a pity.

Because the termination of post-parole support groups for program participants, not coincidentally around the same time Harvard fired Dr. Leary, figures more prominently in the Concord disappointment than psilocybin. The general consensus now is had a greater emphasis been placed on post-parole programs, the psilocybin project would have been a measurable success. Falling victim to the infamous "halo effect," in which researchers tend to see their data in the most positive light, is not uncommon and rarely cause for halting further research, as seems to have happened with psilocybin.

But perhaps the greatest consequence of Concord happened shortly thereafter, when, as Hofmann lamented in *Problem Child,* the irresponsible use of LSD surfaced. Pretend you're Timothy Leary for a minute. You're riding tall in the saddle and looking good on paper. And then you take LSD. You like it a lot. And begin to think if you worked miracles with prisoners on psilocybin, maybe you can save the world with LSD by simply proclaiming turn on, tune in, and drop out. So you do. Boy, do you ever. And boy, were you ever struck blind by the halo effect.

Not to speak ill of the fallen, as there is some heroic notion in being the first soldier over the hill, due mostly to taking the first bullet, but Timothy Leary made it all sound too easy and too perfect. He never spoke of any downside, and I was a teenager paying attention. And being pretty Catholic at the time, I thought he believed himself a kind of messiah when he formed the League of Spiritual Development. But even later, after taking LSD, and no longer pretty Catholic, I still thought the same.

And yet I can't help thinking now about a short period during the Mysteries, when the sacred potion *kykeon* passed the lips in revelry instead of reverence, rising a bump in the road to Eluesis. The keepers of the secrets weren't happy with such a pagan pursuit, saying, essentially, there is but one true way. Which makes me wonder if that idea sounded as familiar back then as it does today. So perhaps Leary, for all his high crimes and misdemeanors, was our pagan in pursuit of kept secrets. And his only real sin, while riding tall in that saddle, was believing he'd found them all.

Hallucinogens will help you find God. Hallucinogens won't help you find God. Take your pick. But it doesn't really matter. Because whatever path we seek, it is best we accept some among us will illuminate their way with hallucinogens, as they will always remain a certain coin for a certain realm. And may all our journeys be safe. No one knows what lies beyond the final curtain, and I think we'll all be surprised.

Some more than others.

NAKED TRUTH III

Amphetamines

What is right about a society that actively pursues and prosecutes its adult population for the use of a dangerous drug while, simultaneously, promoting and prescribing the same drug to millions of her children? Absolutely nothing.

But that is exactly what is happening.

If a child in your family or in a family you know has been diagnosed with attention deficit disorder/hyperactivity (ADDH), then you know a child who is more than likely taking Ritalin or Adderall. Those drugs are two peas from the same amphetamine pod. Both are powerful and both are addictive. Yet we give them to our children like M&Ms. Every day. Let that soak in for a minute. Okay. Now let's talk about it.

Back in the old days, the phrase "speed kills" had merit. It served to caution those who took amphetamines – long-distance drivers, college students, the bored – of the destructive nature of this powerful drug. And by and large most amphetamine users heeded that message. It appears now the new message is "speed heals." Could this be one time when shooting the messenger makes sense?

Peter R. Breggin M.D. thinks so. As Director of the International Center for the Study of Psychiatry and Psychology, he testified before the U.S. House of Representatives on September 29th, 2000. "My purpose today," Doctor Breggin said to those members of Congress, "is to provide to this committee, parents, teachers, counselors and other concerned adults a scientific basis for rejecting the use of stimulants for the treatment of attention deficit hyperactivity disorder or for the control of behavior in the classroom or home."

But to everyone who thinks the use of amphetamine-grade stimulants to control our children is a current phenomenon, or controversy, think again. It was back in the 50s when stimulant drugs were first approved for child behavior control. And between then and the 70s, Dr. Breggin further testified, "there have been periodic attempts to promote their usage, and periodic public reactions against the practice. In fact," he added, "the first Congressional hearings critical of stimulant medication were held in the early 70s when an estimated 100,000-200,000 children were receiving these drugs."

A 1998 study published in the Journal of the American Medical Association found the number of children taking stimulants in 1985 had risen to 570,000, nearly tripling the 70s number. The total in 1994, just nine years later, was 2,860,000, a five-fold increase. And today the total is even higher. So what is responsible for the explosion?

A variety of things, it seems. But uppermost of all indicators is that parents across the country are under heavy pressure from schools to medicate their children into better learning, or at least to sit tight until the final bell rings at the end of the school day. What makes the pressure work is the deft playing on, then playing off, parental guilt. You're not made to believe Johnny's problem is your fault, but it helps to sell the deal if they let you think about it a little. And you do.

Classifying non-conforming behavior in the classroom as a disease (ADDH) is the current medical premise for prescribing stimulant drugs as the cure. The ADDH diagnosis, appearing in the 1994 Diagnostic and Statistical Manual of Mental Disorders of the American Psychiatric Association, conferred all requisite credibility to continue medicating our children. (The need to legitimize such a controversial and widespread practice was an important point Dr. Breggin hoped would not be lost on Congress.)

And there seems consensus U.S. children consume nearly 85% of all stimulant drugs produced – over 8 *tons* a year – to treat ADDH. Certain logic would follow that our world ranking in education should benefit from such brain doping, just as an Olympic athlete taking steroids generally outperforms competitors who do not. But that's not the case. Why? Well, it just might be due to how the stimulant affects the child.

Again, Dr. Breggin. "First, the drugs suppress all spontaneous behavior. This is manifested in a reduction in the following behaviors: exploration and curiosity, socializing and playing. Second, the drugs increase obsessive-compulsive behaviors." Hmmm... Call me crazy, but suppressing behaviors beneficial to learning while increasing those detrimental does not seem to be the best recipe for classroom success.

I reference Dr. Peter Breggin for two reasons. First, he provides an articulate and persuasive argument for those who advocate ending childhood stimulant use. Second, because it is additional documented testimony given before Congress. And for that, our elected leaders cannot feign ignorance. But there are two sides to every story. So let's hear the other side.

Pharmaceutical companies and those in the medical community involved in medicating our children are natural proponents. And they too present a persuasive, if not quite unbiased, argument. But rather than dwell on them, I'll relate what I've learned from those on the stimulant front-lines, those parents and teachers in the trenches.

Many but not all teachers I have spoken with tend to side with the pharmaceutical and medical community. But their allegiance is tinged with an air of resignation, as if the practice of medicating their students is just a band-aid on a rupturing jugular. And such a practice, they tell me, is less about fomenting better education and more centered on maintaining classroom discipline.

And a lot of teachers are just scared to death, plain and simple. My mother is a retired schoolteacher, and thanks God daily she no longer is in the fray. She saw the discipline problem coming and feels the issue falls squarely upon the shoulders of parents. Her more than thirty years standing in front of the blackboard convinced her education was a two-pronged attack.

And it starts in the home. Central to parental responsibility is the establishment of accountability and respect. Children must be taught, at home, that their actions do not reside in a vacuum, but rather in a setting of action/reaction. And that respect for others is the surest way to earn respect. Those are learned rather than intuitive responses, as anyone can witness by observing young children at play.

Parents, at least the vast majority of those I've spoken with, agree. And work diligently toward that goal. But a number of these caring parents are at a loss. Life has become more complicated. Most every single parent works, as do most two-parent households. Time, quality or otherwise, is at a premium. And has become, for better and oftentimes worse, another factor in the decision to give their children stimulants.

A family close to me has a child diagnosed with ADD. Their decision to try Ritalin was not easily made. And though they believe it was beneficial in the immediate sense of improving their child's behavior and opportunity to learn, the dearth of empirical data regarding Ritalin's longer-term effect makes for uneasy peace of mind. Like many parents, they are aware studies indicate childhood use of Ritalin may predispose users to substance abuse as adults.

It seems odd that the medical community, while appearing united in the belief drug addiction is a disease, can square the prescription of addictive drugs to children, some for many years. But at the end of the day, whether you support stimulant use, oppose it or are uneasy with your child taking these drugs, they are being legally prescribed and given to millions of our children, many having little say in the process. But let's take the amphetamine debate out of the schools and put it into the adult world where it belongs. Where, at the very least, you needn't be told twice to take your medicine.

So, was JFK a junkie?

Of course, the recent dustup over president Kennedy shooting drugs in the White House was characterized more delicately as a concern over "impairment." Semantics. I figure if it walks like a duck and quacks like a duck, a duck is what you've got. But I'm not really hunting ducks here. However, the context does present an opportune point to begin the discussion of adult amphetamine use.

Americans recently learned the full extent of our former president's debilitations, and the pharmaceutical solutions employed to ease them. Though JFK's meds were many, as were his afflictions, his narcotic use generated the most media buzz: he took opiates for pain. And as someone with chronic back pain only partially corrected by surgery, I'm a firm believer in opiate therapy. But I'm also convinced opiates tend to dull the senses.

Senses, the kind necessary to be sharp in the event, say, the world is faced with nuclear war. Not all of you were around during the Cuban missile crisis, but the world faced just such a dilemma. Nikita Khrushchev, that shoe-pounding Soviet premier, had secretly placed nuclear missiles in Cuba. When a chagrined Kennedy White House demanded Khrushchev remove them, a dangerous world became even more so.

Toss in an opiated president injecting amphetamines to stay focused, and the whole thing takes on the surreal essence of Salvador Dali's *Hallucinogenic Toreador*. But to make a long story short, Khrushchev blinked. Which makes perfect sense when you think about it, as Kennedy was probably too wired to close his eyes, let alone blink. And the world stepped back from the brink. So, if Kennedy was "impaired," that's my kind of impairment.

If you're keeping score, so far it's our kids and a past president taking amphetamines for the better good. Let's make it three for three and talk about Air Force fighter pilots. It took America's "friendly fire" killing of four Canadian soldiers in Afghanistan to expose the quiet practice of prescribing amphetamines to U.S. Air Force pilots. But you can bet flight surgeons of every air force in every country follow suit. It makes sense: when you are at the controls of a highly sophisticated multi-million dollar military aircraft, dozing off in the wild blue yonder presents ample opportunity for calamity.

As reported by the Associated Press, David Beck, a lawyer for F-16 pilot Major William Umbach, implied the "go pills" issued to his client may have impaired his judgment. So, like many, I watched the TV when images of the pilot's pop-up display and video view of the action were played. But I paid particular attention to the audio, listening for any clue indicating the pilot may have been "hopped-up" on speed. His voice seemed restrained, even calm, even at the end when he somberly wondered aloud if he had done the right thing.

As it turns out, he didn't. But I'm not so sure his future should be ruined, as will probably be the case. Nor do I believe amphetamines played a causative role, yet there is no question his fighter-pilot days are over. For years, and possibly the rest of his life, William Umbach will find little comfort in those dark and reflective moments just before sleep, which seems consequence enough. One can only hope it will be consequence enough for the bereaved families.

Our kids, a president and pilots: three different examples of legal amphetamine use. Yet whether in the classroom, the White House or the cockpit, each has the same bottom line to keep the user focused. And it is that same bottom line which fuels most illegal amphetamine use. I know it fueled mine, although I took them only a handful or so times.

My friend Bob liked speed a whole lot more than I did. Bob was over six foot and about 180 lbs, hardly overweight, but that didn't stop his hometown doctor from prescribing them nearly two years for just such a problem. And Bob was not alone in obtaining amphetamines this way. I knew more than a few slim co-eds doing the same thing.

Because amphetamines were de rigueur for frequent "all-nighters." Many college students would boogie the term away in an alcoholic stupor, confident the last few days before finals could be spent in amphetamine-fueled cramming. Not all of our future leaders of America had access to such pharmaceutical study aids, a fact reflected in campus drug stores stocking multiple over-the-counter products specifically designed to keep the sandman at bay. (Come on, you took 'em. Fess-up.)

Like I said, I'm guilty – if that's the proper term – of taking amphetamines while in college. Passing a Geology 201 final may not equate with the Cuban missile crisis or determining friend or foe from ten thousand feet, yet it certainly seems in concert with the stated purpose behind giving our school children Ritalin.

But it was often a pig in a poke when college students bought amphetamines. I was lucky. Bob's came fresh from the pharmacy. So I knew precisely what drug I was doing and, more importantly, the exact dosage. That could never be said of bathtub speed, and there was a lot of that around. And I suspect it's the same now.

Except college kids today are not eating pharmaceutical diet pills. Ritalin is all over the black market. Much of it is stolen from pharmacies. But a good supply comes from the prescribed children. Kids game the system. But at least, as even Doctor Breggin may concede, adults are taking the drugs. Which bears repeating my opening question: What is right about a society that actively pursues and prosecutes its adult population for the use of a dangerous drug while, simultaneously, promoting and prescribing the same drug to millions of her children?

No adult enjoys being treated like a child, yet perhaps this is one instance where the practice would not be all that objectionable. That's because amphetamines act upon everyone's central nervous system in just about the same way, whether handed out by the school nurse or your best friend. Thinking otherwise is naïve. Millions of us have taken amphetamines and, in the main, suffered little as a result. That being said, I'd rather be locked in the basement with a hundred heroin addicts than one speed freak. And I've known a few. They weren't really dangerous, just way too busy.

And the exception to the responsible use theory. Amphetamine abuse is a serious problem, but restricted to a very small number of individuals. Aggressive tendencies exacerbated by amphetamines pose difficulties for society, without question, but nearly all the crime and violence stems directly from the black market, something the repeal of drug prohibition will quickly eliminate. And it may very well decrease amphetamine use, in a phenomenon known as "drug switching."

Amphetamines have been around since first synthesized in 1887 Germany. And there are reports soldiers on both sides of world wars were supplied amphetamines to improve stamina and, as a result, be more effective at killing their enemy. Outside of this military practice, amphetamine use had very little recreational appeal. Those who enjoyed the effects of stimulants used cocaine, considered the better drug. Amphetamine use rose in popularity simply because cocaine was banned by the Harrison Narcotics Act of 1914. Amphetamines remained legal. So it is not out of the question – or splitting hairs – to suggest cocaine, with the repeal of drug prohibition, will regain favor with the stimulant set.

But the most important issue remains whether or not we should continue prescribing amphetamines to our young children. Do we accept what many consider effective short-term success in lieu of the potential long-term failure? I'm not sure. The debate is fifty years old and likely to continue, with as many fingers crossed over the outcome as we cross on lottery night. Yet it is impossible to trust giving our children amphetamines will not lead thousands into adult addiction. And it is absolutely Orwellian to know we will hunt them down like dogs when they do.

Sleep tight, everyone.

NAKED TRUTH IV

Barbiturates

"Take two aspirin and call me in the morning." That old saying is familiar to just about everyone. Probably not so familiar is that a pharmaceutical company headed by Adolph von Bayer discovered aspirin, a drug beneficial to an overwhelming majority of users. Not a bad day's work. And those scientists von Bayer employed were a busy lot. They also gave the world heroin.

But it was Adolph von Bayer himself, in 1863, that first synthesized barbituric acid. It was a combination of urea (found in your urine) and malonic acid (common in unripe fruit), and formed the base material of barbiturates. Adolph von Bayer made his synthesized discovery on the feast day for Saint Barbara, and so named his discovery in her honor (the suffix urates is uric acid salt). A rather dubious honor, as no practical application was found for barbiturates, so Adolph put them in a drawer somewhere.

Forty years later, in 1903, barbital was synthesized and introduced as Veronal, a sedative. And those suffering terminal nervousness found a friend. So did insomniacs, epileptics, and mental patients fogged by long-term hospitalization, as well as jittery patients awaiting surgery. It was a winner. All told, there were some 2,500 derivatives of von Bayer's original barbiturate discovery – all considered wonder drugs of their day.

Except it turned out barbiturates were highly addictive; that ugly fly in medicinal ointments. Barbiturates affect gamma-aminobutyric acid (GABA) receptors, bringing about an overall inhibition of the central nervous system, affecting the part of your brain stem responsible for regulating the rhythms of wake and sleep. The result of such inhibition is getting knocked-out. Take two and call me when you wake-up.

If you do, that is. When taken in excess, that common pitfall of "if one is good, two must be better," barbiturates present life-and-death scenarios. And when washed down with a martini or any other alcoholic concoction, as was often the case, death loomed over life in precarious fashion. That mix produced deeper levels of intoxication, as well as greatly lowering blood pressure and heart rates, leading to cardiovascular collapse. And long-term barbiturate users suffer similar scenarios when deciding to go cold turkey. It's not pretty, folks.

All of which did nothing, however, to slow the prescriptions written for barbiturates. Neither did the display of nasty behaviors exhibited by chronic barbiturate users. Irritability and aggressive tendencies were common, as well as lethargy, confusion and the crying at the drop of a hat.

Helps shed light on some of the more unfathomable actions of our parents and grandparents, huh?

But they didn't have all the fun. No sir. It wasn't long before the recreational use of barbiturates entered their scene. Yet the desire to stay awake and have fun was counterintuitive to the sedative nature of barbiturates, and produced an awkward intoxication. You weren't really asleep, but should have been. Inhibitions were relaxed, naturally, but toss in a drink or two and they disappeared. Many advantages were taken in this circumstance, and by both sets of chromosomes.

Variations of that theme were played when my generation took their turn in the barbiturate barrel. And speed freaks I knew loved and craved them as cushions against the eventual hard amphetamine crash. Witnessing both probably contributed to my early passing whenever offered. But let's keep in mind curiosity doesn't kill every cat.

Watching a body advance through the various stages of a barbiturate load can make for an interesting evening. There is a distinct difference in folks who take them with booze instead of water. Those who mix in alcohol are the most foolish and tend to flame brighter but briefer. And if your natural tendency leans toward being a mean drunk, barbiturates are not exactly a mellowing agent.

But not everybody was an idiot. Much of the recreational barbiturate use traveling my orbits did not involve alcohol. Nor was it a big drug of choice. We may have looked stupid, but many of us were not ignorant. We took more than a passing interest in pharmacology, wanting a firm handle on what we were putting into our bodies. The general consensus, backed by personal experience and observational judgment on peer abuse, was that barbiturates were a losing proposition.

Long-term barbiturate addicts spared an ignominious death face life with impaired thinking, reduced motor skills, depression and paranoia. And, as if that's not enough, reduced sex-drive. Evidence of such fun side effects notwithstanding, the medical community was slow to lessen reliance upon iterations of Bayer's Saint Barbara's urates. What they needed was a new drug. And it was in 1963 when they found one, aptly memorialized in song by the Rolling Stones as "mother's little helper."

NAKED TRUTH IVa
Benzodiazepine

It may be "only rock and roll," but Glimmer Twins Mick and Keith hit the nail squarely on the head with their lyrical description of Valium. Indeed it was "mother's little helper." And was considered the Holy Grail among those in pharmaceutical circles searching for a barbiturate replacement. Yet it wasn't discovered as much as found by Doctor Alec Jenner, a young and ambitious psychiatrist in England. More accurately, he read about it in the newspaper.

It was in the local *Daily Mirror*. And it was a story telling of an animal trainer using benzodiazepine as a tiger sedative. Though none of Jenner's patients displayed ferocities near that of a tiger, some were quite impervious to available treatments. Perhaps it was those he had in mind when suggesting to colleagues how the tiger sedative "could work on the people of Sheffield," a local psychiatric hospital. They thought he was joking.

He wasn't. Doctor Alec Jenner sensed an opportunity and, seeking it, wrote Swiss pharmaceutical company Hoffmann La Roche. His correspondence proffered the idea benzodiazepine could be beneficial to humans with anxiety issues, and made the case for his carrying out patient trials. Always on the lookout for the "next big thing" in drug therapy, Hoffmann La Roche agreed to sponsor Doctor Jenner's patient trials. When those trials proved encouraging, Roche developed Valium. And a star was born.

Valium was trumpeted to the world in 1963 and became legendary for its positive effect on persons suffering anxiety and depression. Millions of prescriptions were written across the globe. And many millions are being written yet today. However, as with barbiturates, Valium carried the baggage of addiction. This was recognized early on but, again, did nothing to slow the prescription flow.

Well-intentioned doctors cautioned their patients that Valium should be taken for only short periods of time. But few physicians were willing to deny their patients numerous refills. After all, finding another, more agreeable doctor was not all that difficult. Neither was finding a sympathetic friend: Valium was traded among adults with the same nonchalance as baseball cards among kids.

One would think Doctor Jenner, now in is 70s and retired, should feel a certain pride in his accomplishment. But he doesn't. Jenner now admits to a certain naiveté over not considering the dependency issue while conducting his benzodiazepine trials. In the rush to replace barbiturates, such research was minimal and not all that conducive to the profit-making plans of pharmaceutical companies.

"Long-term trials are very expensive and difficult to arrange," Doctor Jenner said in a November 2000 interview. And "you cannot take this out of the equation in assessing what happened with benzodiazepines." He added: "I would have been surprised if Roche had asked me to do long-term trials of Valium. This is where you can be critical of the drug companies – but not the system in which they work."

Maybe.

For in the first decade of benzodiazepine use, the World Health Organization and the British Medical Journal, parts of the "system," identified the drug as one of dependence. Yet it wasn't until 1988, when a class-action suit brought against benzodiazepine manufacturers, that the Committee of Safety of Medicines recognized the addictive nature of benzodiazepine.

Yet Valium remains readily available, but is now considered passé. For doctors and patients wanting to be on the cutting edge of anxiety medication, Xanax is the latest, greatest thing. Like Valium, Xanax is a benzodiazepine, differing only in how fast it takes effect and how long it lasts (known as the drug's half-life). Such designer drugs may be the pride of pharmaceutical companies, and their stockholders, but the fact remains benzodiazepines are addictive substances.

It is not my field of expertise or my desire to hold forth on why we are such an anxious people, but without a doubt we are. Though, for my money, a little meditation and breathing exercises would go a long way in helping those among us deal with the stresses of everyday life. Of course, that's a lot harder than popping a pill or two.

Less you feel I'm being sanctimonious, my generation did not escape their dance with downers. Not by a long shot, baby. But being the rebellious generation, we rejected barbiturates and benzodiazepines, not being crazy for anything our parents liked. So we found our own drug. And it wasn't anxiety that spurred the search. It was the ants in our pants.

NAKED TRUTH IVb
Methaqualone

First synthesized in 1955, in India, by M.L. Gujral, and long before Jenner had his tiger epiphany, methaqualone was introduced as a safe barbiturate alternative. Ten years later it was the most commonly prescribed sedative in Britain, while quickly becoming a popular recreational drug. And by 1972 methaqualone became a top-selling sedative in the United States. Another no real surprise was its wide recreational use once it hopped across the pond.

Quaaludes. The love drug millions of baby boomers deny doing, feeling their sheepish admission of "experimenting" with pot while in youthful pursuits conjures up enough of a picture. Having crazy "lude" sex with the lights on in a room of others similarly engaged is the Polaroid missing from many a family album. Which is a good thing, because we'd recognize a lot of faces.

Quaalude use transcended the hippie/straight divisions. Folks who wouldn't be caught dead smoking a joint would eat a Quaalude or two without batting an eye. Granted, we may not have been at the same party but we were pretty much doing the same thing: screwing our brains out. It was *the* love drug. And it seemed there was an awful lot of love going around, at least in the 70s and early 80s.

It was the Rorer 714 Quaalude that most personifies that time. Developed in the 60s by William H. Rorer, Inc., then best known for the antacid *Maalox,* it contained 300 milligrams of methaqualone and was sold as a sedative. Choosing the trademark Quaalude was a clever bit of marketing: inserting the familiar *aa* of *Maalox* into a contraction of *quiet interlude* produced a subliminally seductive word. Not that the drug needed the help, mind you.

But for real aficionados, the earlier days of the Sopor are those most wistfully remembered. Sopor was the trade name given to the Arnor Stone Co. product containing the same 300 milligrams of methaqualone as the Rorer 714. But for anyone who has taken both, Sopors get the pun intended nod. Maybe it was because they came first, or the fact they were orange. Or maybe its cult status was created by a *60 Minutes* segment devoted to the anomaly of a drug phenomenon originating not on either of the hipper coasts, but in the Midwest heartland.

And boy, did we take that drug to heart.

The orange Sopor craze hit the Ohio State University campus like a freight train, as railroad workers played a significant role in creating the market. Back pain was a common malady among railroad hands, resulting in many a sleepless night. Given a Sopor prescription, one sufferer raved about the restive results to his fellow rail workers, and piqued the interest of an OSU student working there part-time.

The story goes that the student wrangled a couple of Sopors from his overjoyed co-worker. An enterprising fellow, he quickly realized the recreational potential. Hooking up with a friend working as a summer intern at a major drug chain's warehouse in another Ohio city, many 55-gallon drums of Sopors were surreptitiously diverted to the black market. And another star, at least according to *60 Minutes,* was born.

I came across Sopors when returning to OSU after being cleared of my first encounter with policeman Murrill Johnson. I moved into a large house with my friend Bob and three other nice folks, plus a goofy Great Dane. It was the owner of the house, a college dropout rehabbing houses for campus-area landlords, who just so happened to know a guy who knew a guy who worked on the railroad.

It was years after I left Ohio that I came to know about his connection. And that helped explain the thorough third degree he gave me before taking my rent money. Remember, as someone recently busted for drugs, I trailed the whiff of uncertainty of allegiance. When finally satisfied I was just another hapless hippie, he threw an impromptu welcoming party. And gave me my first Sopor. It wasn't the last one I would take.

The effect was very nice. My body was all tingly and quite relaxed; the quintessential warm and fuzzy feeling. It was like being drunk but only from the neck down, as my mental clarity seemed little changed. Which is why I believe girls liked them so much. It would render them loose as a goose, yet largely in control of their sexual choices. And that awkward morning after, the bane of alcohol-fogged passions of the night, rarely transpired.

It was a fun drug. And, as drugs go, widely considered pretty safe in moderate use. Frequent recreational use built a certain tolerance but not physical addiction. I should know. Sopors, at least in 1971 and 1972, were not all that hard to come by. We enjoyed them when available, and availability was such that addiction had its opportunity. It is just that I rarely saw it being seized.

Sopors ended up a quick blip on the methaqualone radar screen: gone by 1973. But not to worry, the Rorer 714 Quaalude roared into town. Which is when the party really started for most folks. DEA publications (www.dea.gov/deamuseum/1980-1985) state methaqualone use soared dramatically before the decade's end. William H. Rorer, Inc., even had it wanted to, could not meet such demand. Which produced the great irony of Quaalude use: many folks never experienced a real Rorer 714. They took counterfeits, or "bootlegs" to the trade.

All courtesy of the Colombian drug cartels. By and large very bad people, but they sure could spot a trend. And they weren't bad at reading handwriting on the wall, either. When the DEA initiated global curbs on methaqualone powder production, the cartels conspired to buy up much of the world's supply, and largely succeeded. They flooded the market with bootlegs, making enormous profits. DEA estimates were that 85% of the Quaaludes consumed in the early 80s, considered the peak of use, were counterfeits.

Where the drug cartels largely failed, however, was in the area of quality control. Some bootlegs were hard to spot, but most were not. They were crudely pressed and crumbled easily. And it was the rare bootleg that actually contained the precise Rorer benchmark of 300 milligrams of methaqualone. Cheaper, filler ingredients – some benign, some not – were often used, and many bootlegs lacked even the smallest amount of methaqualone.

Which radically altered the dynamics of dosing. Any given batch of 100 bootlegs was likely to include widely dis-

parate levels of potency, creating dangerous Quaalude roulette scenarios for the user. And was no doubt a contributing
factor to abuse and overdose. DEA documents cite a Drug
Abuse Warning Network (DAWN) survey, using emergency
room visits as just one indicator, that reports methaqualone
abuse increased 40% in 1979 alone.

Abuse I witnessed in both friends and acquaintances. But
nearly every dependency involved concurrent abuse of other
drugs, most notably alcohol (as is the case today). Which is
a predicament of character flaw or genetic predisposition;
take your pick. Yet that hardly matters, as each theory in
practice produces pretty much the same addict and presents
behaviors underscoring the basic premise drugs are not for
everyone.

The rest of us did drugs for fun – simple as that. And
moved on when the thrill was gone, resulting in not much
harm and very little foul. But it was sometime during that
passing phase stage where certain individuals, for whatever
reason you pick, stayed put. And, quite frankly, ruined a
(qualifiedly) good thing.

At the onset of the 80s, in an attempt to thwart the Colombian cartels, the DEA Diversion Control Program and
our State Department coordinated global efforts to place
more stringent controls on foreign production and exporta-
tion of methaqualone. Yet it would be nearly four years,
years the cartels acquired methaqualone almost at will, before those efforts bore fruit.

By 1984, the United Nations reported just two foreign
countries still engaged in methaqualone production. That
same year the U.S. Congress placed methaqualone into
Schedule I of the CSA, effectively eliminating domestic production and medical use. Here was an effective sedative,

arguably safer than the barbiturates it was intended to replace, driven from the marketplace in order to "save our nation's youth."

Anyone else notice a pattern here?

Perhaps this is one time when stating the obvious makes sense: alcohol is an addictive drug. Certain behaviors under the influence of alcohol are rightfully against the law. Yet alcoholics are not criminalized in our society, for they constitute the exception to the widely held responsible use theory. A theory universally discredited when applied to responsible use of all other addictive drugs.

And just how responsible is that?

NAKED TRUTH V

MDMA

Psychotherapists first named the drug Adam, but today everybody just calls it Ecstasy.

As is true of many drugs, methylenedioxymethamphetamine was the by-product of an attempt to synthesize another medicinal compound. In the case of MDMA, the drug synthesized was Hydrastinin, a vasoconstrictive and styptic drug (designed to compress blood vessels and stem blood flow). This occurred in 1912. Though not a substance subjected to human trials at the time, MDMA, as a part of the synthesizing protocol, was routinely patented two years later by the German drug company Merck.

And routinely ignored until the 50s, when the CIA got into the game, along with the US Army. The CIA game plan once again sought that elusive truth serum. The Army just wanted to know if it could kill you. Rumor has it the CIA, as they did with LSD, found MDMA wanting. But it would kill you, Army research concluded, though the lethal dose was impracticably high, somewhere in the 1500-milligram range. So for both mental and physical warfare, MDMA seemed of no value.

All this was kept hushed until the early 70s, when the CIA published their research findings. But it's no secret psychotherapists like to play in the same sandbox with psychoactive drugs, especially those that can't hurt you. After all, *do no harm* is the first tenet of the Hippocratic oath. Learning of MDMA, psychotherapists soon discovered that ingesting 125 milligrams of pure and unadulterated MDMA made you feel very, very good. Which was something they felt would be extremely helpful to those with mental trauma, whether self-inflicted or imposed. Here's why.

Serotonin is the chemical your body produces to make you feel good. Literally. Serotonin is made at the base of the brain in the raphe nucleus, and then stored in axons. Axons are the brain's intrastate system, reaching all the far corners. And your synapse is the brain's off-ramp leading to your every nerve. So when the brain sees the need here or there for a little squirt of well-being, delivery is swift and balanced: just enough for most folks to climb out of bed every morning and face the day's music.

But when the music of everyday life devolves into constant cacophony, the resulting mental trauma may interfere with the brain's command and control center to upset the normal serotonin flow. Or it may not. It may be that the normal flow of serotonin just can't beat a bad case of the blues. But either way you slice it, serotonin was not doing its job. It needed help, help supplied by MDMA.

MDMA triggers an immediate release of all stored serotonin into the synapse, flooding your central nervous system with a near overwhelming rush of well-being, just what the doctor ordered. Patient response was ecstatic and many felt several days of MDMA sessions outpaced several years of regular therapy. And had its use stayed within the province of psychotherapy, MDMA would no doubt today be a valuable therapeutic drug. But it didn't, and is not. And some folks should be ashamed of themselves. For when all the dust settles and you blow it away, MDMA works for the wounded and will enhance the well.

Yet it is certainly true the existing evidence can hardly be considered empirical. To be thought so requires ongoing study, something denied MDMA. Denied when the matter of scheduling MDMA under the Controlled Substances Act came before the United States Department of Justice in 1984. Presiding as Administrative Law Judge was Francis L. Young.

A redaction of the entire rule making proceeding can be found at www.mninter.net/~publish/mdma. You won't be surprised to read MDMA was placed on Schedule I of the Controlled Substances Act, effectively shutting down all medical research and creating the Catch-22 of MDMA empirical data collection: you can't do the research if you can't do the drug. But what Administrative Law Judge Francis Young actually ruled may be a surprise, and how it all came to be will be clearer with a little background perspective.

So what say we take a trip down memory lane to see just how MDMA came to earn its pariah status. We know the CIA didn't like it (they wanted to hear secrets, not "I love you, man...wanna dance?"). And the Army determined consuming a pill the size of a hockey puck was needed to kill you, something even the most gullible enemy would find hard to swallow. So MDMA was rejected: it can't be any good if it can't be bad.

But what if the reverse – if it ain't bad it might be good – were true? Perhaps that may well have inspired Alexander Shulgin some thirty years ago to experiment with MDMA. A respected biochemist by trade, Shulgin wrote and published the first scientific article accrediting the effects of MDMA. Aside from finding MDMA better than any martini at a cocktail party, Shulgin, now in his 70s, had a strong inkling of the drug's therapeutic value. And gave samples to you know who: psychotherapists.

And we know they liked it. So did close to 4,000 of their patients. One enterprising patient believed Adam might benefit the masses if allowed to step outside the doctor's office. So he hired a chemist and opened an MDMA lab in Dallas, Texas. Instincts sensed the name Adam wouldn't do. Empathy was first considered, as it was the most descriptive, but wasn't very sexy and quickly discarded in favor of ecstasy. (A bit of overselling, if you ask me, but a stroke of marketing genius.)

With production up and running, our patient/entrepreneur sold batches of ecstasy tablets to all the local hip and trendy watering holes in Dallas. They in turn sold it to all their hip and trendy patrons for twenty bucks a pop, plus tax. You could even charge it to your American Express card (and against your expense report?). Anyway, sales were all above board and legal and very brisk.

And a godsend, it appears, to not only the troubled and the trendy of Dallas but to the onward Christian soldiers attending Southern Methodist University across town. Prohibited by their religion from drinking alcohol, students were known to find certain salvation in taking ecstasy. And you can bet more than a few shouts of "Praise the Lord" were offered up for their ecstasy enthrallments. Can I get an Amen (and a little drum roll for the irony)?

Word quickly spread throughout much of Texas. Ecstasy became very popular, with gross receipts in some hip and trendy joints approaching those for alcohol. MDMA labs mushroomed to supply this demand. Ecstasy's mainstream appeal traveled well, turning up in other states. Without the hallucinogenic effect of LSD or the wired-tight aspect of cocaine or, the main highlight, alcohol's hangover, ecstasy was to many the perfect party favor.

But the agony of ecstasy wasn't far behind. The 1984 Amendment to the Controlled Substances Act included a provision sponsored by the DEA to grant them authority to invoke "immediate scheduling" of any new drug not found to be in the public interest. Without such authority, the then current, more formal process of drug scheduling could take several years. Still smarting from the sneak attack of crack cocaine, the DEA was not about to be blindsided by ecstasy.

So the DEA invoked their new discretionary power over MDMA, July 1, 1985. Their evidence was sketchy knowledge of private MDMA labs churning out ecstasy pills, along with a strong suspicion citizens were having more fun than the law should allow. Not only that, Your Honor, some bar patrons were vomiting. Kudos, I think, to the DEA agent who can distinguish ecstasy spew from the hurl of one too many Heinekens.

But the powers that be triumphed, stitching fear to the hearts of psychotherapists. The clinical use of Adam ceased almost immediately, laying waste the promise of further breakthrough. Imagine the added trauma to a troubled mind when told Adam had been banished from the pharmacopoeia garden. The biblical correlation is just too eerie to write about, but do think on it for a minute.

While these pioneering psychotherapists feared government scrutiny, lay practitioners did not, taking up the MDMA cause. One fellow with independent wealth and enough confidence not to be intimidated was Rick Doblin. He first took MDMA in 1982, when it was still legal. And as founder of the Multidisciplinary Association for Psychedelic Studies (MAPS), Doblin remains a passionate and well-versed advocate of MDMA's therapeutic importance. Though using MAPS to "study ways to take drugs to open the unconscious" makes him a little touchy-feely for some, Doblin and MAPS have funded important MDMA research.

One recipient of MAPS money was Johns Hopkins neurotoxicologist George Ricaurte. His research concluded serotonin levels are diminished after just one ecstasy pill. In animals, that is. Of course animal trials have paid the freight for much benefit, yet sometimes there is nothing like the real thing. So Ricuarte knew human trials were needed.

But with MDMA demonized then outlawed by the DEA, obtaining the drug was legally impossible. So Ricuarte hit the streets. He didn't buy ecstasy there, but that's where he found his research subjects, seeking volunteers with recent ecstasy experience to undergo memory tests. Ricaurte's control group, those said never to have used ecstasy, tested better. Also, brain scans of the user group reveal fewer serotonin receptors than the control group, leading Ricuarte to believe such damage irreversible.

It is important to understand those with memory loss were not screened for other drug use, including alcohol, which can be assumed more likely than not, and therefore a mitigating factor. More importantly, Ricuarte had no way of knowing if his volunteers, despite their hopes, had actually taken MDMA. His tests were performed in 2000, when street ecstasy often contained other ingredients – some harmless, some not – and sometimes no MDMA at all.

Dr. John Morgan, a professor of pharmacology at the City University of New York (CUNY), also believes the forced release of serotonin poses risks, but accepts the fact millions successfully manipulate serotonin levels daily with Prozac. (Prozac does not release serotonin, it just maximizes levels already delivered by blocking what normally seeps back into the brain.) Yet despite those user brain scans, Morgan states "none of the subjects Ricuarte studied had any evidence of brain or psychological dysfunction."

A point Ricuarte concedes: "The vast majority of people who have experimented with MDMA appear normal, and there's no obvious indication that something is amiss." However, a decade or two down the road may prove otherwise, leading Morgan to concede there remain many "unanswered questions." Answers obtainable through qualitative and quantitative research only, something the DEA deemed a pipe dream.

The aftermath of DEA intervention in 1984 produced two disastrous results. MDMA clinical research was no longer legally possible, stopping important therapeutic advances. And, more to the point, recreational use of ecstasy did not stop. Granted, the initial chill of illegality moved ecstasy from society's mainstream to her fringe. But in less than ten years ecstasy came roaring back to Main Street.

Predictably, ecstasy production became a bastion for greedy bootleggers. Established foreign drug cartels and our homegrown mobsters joined forces to supply surging demand. But quality control in bootleg ecstasy, as with Quaaludes, was virtually non-existent. Like the volunteers in Ricuarte's study, ecstasy users today can only hope for the best. And it is mostly those whose hopes go unfulfilled that end up in hospitals – and sometimes the morgue.

Despite DEA best efforts, ecstasy remains readily available. I can have it delivered to my home nearly as fast as any pizza. Yet, and largely because of those same DEA efforts, the likelihood my pepperoni is real exceeds greatly that of the ecstasy. In fact, a November 2000 research letter to the Journal of the American Medical Association (JAMA) addresses the chemical analysis of ecstasy pills. A detailed assay of 107 ecstasy samples, from coast-to-coast and Hawaii, found thirty-one (29%) had no MDMA at all, and that nine others (8%) contained no identifiable drug.

So, right out of the chute, the chances of getting *any* MDMA in your ecstasy are less than one in three. And, according to that JAMA letter, the remaining sixty-seven pills (63%) contained other drugs in combination with some MDMA. There was caffeine, ephedrine, pseudoephedrine and salicylates, but in amounts not shown to produce significant toxicity. The most common – and most toxic – adulterant found in twenty-three pills (21%) was dextromethorphan (DXM).

Designed to relieve or suppress coughing, the usual therapeutic dose of DXM is just 15 to 30 milligrams. Those twenty-three ecstasy samples assayed contained a range from 103 to 211 milligrams of DXM, averaging 136 each. And as many ecstasy users today consume multiple pills, often at once, the DXM content can be much greater than 300 milligrams. Such high levels can make one very lazy or way too busy, or absolutely spastic and fear a heartbeat so fast your eyeballs actually bounce. And, in some cases, question what planet you're on.

Which sounds like most everybody ever rushed to emergency rooms and diagnosed with ecstasy abuse. But it is of pertinent interest to note DXM goes undetected in standard toxicology screening tests on such patients. So it is highly probable, as suggested by that JAMA letter, dextromethorphan intoxication, and not MDMA, plays the primary causative role in most emergencies. All the while it's a pretty safe bet few if any patients taking Adam suffered similar adverse reactions.

I know I didn't.

But, then again, I took MDMA even before it was dubbed Adam. It was 1971, during spring quarter of my OSU junior year. Two premed students and an aspiring ballerina, all three living in the same apartment building with Bob and me, came to us one day with a tale of a new drug they swore was better than acid. Which, given our fascination with LSD at the time, seemed high praise indeed.

It's vague to me now as to where they got the MDMA (I can't remember *everything* from those heady days...). But based on their enthusiastic gushing over how incredibly great it made you feel, we decided to give it a shot. They had six pills, so we invited the guy down the hall to join in our little experiment. We each took one MDMA tablet and waited for the fun to begin.

The MDMA took about half an hour to come on. Unlike LSD, or any other drug for that matter, there was no pre-game show, that is, no hint the drug was beginning to take effect. It was as if someone just turned on a light switch. All of a sudden a massive rush of serotonin-induced euphoria engulfed our senses and, just as advertised, it was unlike anything we'd experienced before. We danced around like kindergarten kids and truly thought all was right with the world. It lasted but a few hours, but boy, what a great buzz.

And though just acquaintances before taking the MDMA, we all came away with nicer appreciations for each other. (I lost touch with the dancer when she moved out, and one student transferred away. Another ended up my paddy wagon partner later that July. One is my oldest friend. And Bob, sadly, is gone.) After that one-hit wonder day, I never saw or even heard of MDMA again. But I never forgot it.

And it would be another thirty years, New Year's Eve 2001 to be exact, before I had the experience again. Except now MDMA was called ecstasy and the province of the Rave Culture – and #1 with a bullet on the DEA hit list. But what relegated my interest in this "new" drug to just following its exploits in the media was the disturbing trend, ala bootleg Quaaludes, of ecstasy roulette.

Yet the pleasure of real deal MDMA made many college-age ravers feel the risk buying from a stranger worth the taking and believe bad things happened only to the other guy. But they were happening. So not wanting to foul a beautiful old memory kept me on the sidelines during ecstasy's resurgent glory days.

So I'm not entirely certain what convinced me and our little cast of revelers to trade the traditional New Year's Eve LSD experience for ecstasy. Maybe it was September 11th residual doom and gloom. Maybe it was because we trusted the girl who provided the ecstasy. Or maybe after tripping ten year-ends away we were ready for a change. Anyway, we took the ecstasy.

And, for me, it was a near carbon copy of that spring day in 1971. Over the course of 2001's last hours and the first few of 2002, we all played and danced and had a wonderful celebration. All the fun drugs are more fun when you're outside, at least it seems. As it was a beautiful south Florida winter evening, and after watching the ball drop in Times Square, wondering how many of *those* folks were on ecstasy, we took a leisurely bicycle ride through the quiet neighborhoods of my community.

It wasn't a long bike ride – we all had water and peddled like the old people we are – but we all noticed just how extra pretty the palm fronds and pines appeared in the moonlight. It wasn't a hallucination or anything like that at all. But more a subtle reflection of our own heightened senses, feeling, as we did at the time, a little extra pretty ourselves.

We had dodged the ecstasy roulette bullet, but there was a downside. Unlike in 1971, this time multiple tablets were available, and interval dosing extended the experience. (I took the first tablet not long before sunset and the last dose shortly after parking the bicycles, generating almost eight hours of peachy-keen.) Which was great fun but not smart fun. Not smart at all, actually.

That one tablet of MDMA in 1971 produced euphoric states lasting just several hours but left me refreshed and unaffected the next day. New Year's day was different. I felt odd, and near emotionally neutral. And I thought I just might have a case of lockjaw. All of which convinced me my initial experience – one tablet – was the ticket. Call me a party pooper or spoil sport, but that is the most responsible way to enjoy MDMA.

And, of course, insuring the ecstasy you are taking is indeed the real McCoy. But that, as the letter to the JAMA editor confirmed, is a dicey proposition at best. It may seem callous to suggest the DEA is secretly pleased ecstasy users are getting sick – and sometimes dying – but it sure looks that way. "See, I told you so," they seem to be saying. But such smug validation of their dire warnings belies the fact nearly all ecstasy medical emergencies occurred after 1984, when the DEA ended legal (and mostly pure) MDMA production, leaving it in the hands of bathtub bootleggers. The DEA is much like the arsonist fireman rushing heroically into a burning building ignited by his own match.

The real hero in a red hat is a fellow by the name of Bob Wallace. His fire engine is DanceSafe, an organization that tests ecstasy for MDMA content at large dance parties, or "raves," where young folks gather for communal group hugs set to a techno beat. Tables are set up where DanceSafe workers shave a sliver from ecstasy samples. When an applied solution turns the sliver black, MDMA is present. But DanceSafe has found nearly 20% of rave samples contain no MDMA. And when anonymous users send in ecstasy samples from around the U.S. – and when sellers aren't faced with instant karma from ripped-off ravers – DanceSafe has found 40% to be fakes.

Several years ago DanceSafe worked a huge rave in California where nine people were taken away in ambulances. Tests by DanceSafe revealed eight of those nine ravers consumed DXM, and not MDMA. Aside from the wonderful attributes of DXM mentioned earlier, we can add sweat inhibition. Dance for hours while barely breaking a glisten and heatstroke is not uncommon, resulting in that ambulance ride.

Had Bob Wallace's stake in Microsoft (he was employee #9) made him billions instead of millions, DanceSafe would be in more than just a handful of states. As it is, DanceSafe provides aid and comfort to ecstasy users, but swims against an ever-rising tide of greedy and unscrupulous bootleggers. Some bootleggers, and they are that rare exception, actually seek authentication for their product. An honest ecstasy broker can make several hundred thousand dollars a year. Some do much more. And all tax-free.

Even as the honest broker should be valued for certain ethical considerations, his vested interest in an illegal market – keeping fears and prices high – places any value low. Legal MDMA would sell at fractions of today's prices and put ecstasy brokers, honest or not, right out of business. But you know what? They're not even worried. They know MDMA will never again be legal as long as the DEA makes the rules. And with far more ecstasy – good and bad – being consumed than confiscated, dealers and the DEA have become strange bedfellows indeed. Keep those ambulances gassed-up...

So here we are, on a path of society's good intentions that even the blind see as paving the road to hell. We should discredit if not discard conventional wisdoms, especially the aggregate since 1984, for they are indelibly stained with flaws. Legal MDMA research, on the troubled and the well, must renew. Only then can the great promise many feel MDMA holds come to fruition...or not. But let's do begin.

Removing MDMA from Schedule I would be legislatively easy and a fine start. So would employing the responsible use theory, understanding that most recreational users; young adults and even geezers like me, will exercise good judgment. And the overindulgent few, surely to be an issue, as it is with every drug, will at least be spared the ugly consequence of toxic adulterants.

But even when you lump us all together we constitute less than 2% of the population: hardly epidemic proportions. And given ecstasy's ease of access today, a legal MDMA market tomorrow will not greatly expand recreational use, but it undoubtedly will grow. Yet it may well be outgrown, should certain anecdotal evidence gathered during clinical trials of MDMA apply. Two or three MDMA sessions seemed enough to get the therapeutic ball rolling, suggesting maximum benefit is front-loaded.

Which is a theory I find equally credible inside the recreational arena. My own experiences and of others I've polled, suggest a similar law of diminishing returns. Not that the bloom is entirely of the rose, mind you, but replicating initial feelings becomes increasingly more difficult — and less fun: a sure-fire prelude to reduced use. Or maybe it's just notoriously fickle attention spans. Either way, MDMA is destined to remain a niche drug. And fears otherwise are carried by that one-handed man, disallowing "on the other hand" debate to get a grip.

Something Dr. Alexander Shulgin understands quite well, having as he does both hands on the MDMA wheel. Most of you heard first of this man just several pages ago, but DEA and government drug insiders know him very well. After receiving his doctorate in biochemistry, Dr. Shulgin worked for a decade as a senior research chemist for Dow Chemical, inventing profitable products. Departing Dow in 1966 to attend medical school, he stayed just two years: learning how the body and brain worked interested him more than their repair. So he set up a home lab and became a consultant.

Old man Shulgin has been described as a drug-guzzling mad scientist, and that may not be far from the mark. But the DEA is not known for giving madmen drug licenses, something they granted Shulgin around 1968. And maintaining such a license is no easy task: annual scrutiny possessors undergo makes a colonoscopy prep seem like a day at the beach. Yet whatever else Dr. Shulgin was, he was meticulous in his work and able to pass DEA muster for nearly thirty years.

On and off over the next three decades, Dr. Shulgin worked with the DEA, writing the definitive Controlled Substances Act handbook, and testified as an expert witness in DEA drug trials. He also taught forensic toxicology at UC Berkeley and San Francisco State University. And, yes, experimented with a lot of drugs, mostly of his creation. Such taste-testing was no secret to the DEA, a dichotomy lasting until the MDMA dance in Dallas.

Dr. Shulgin had long been a proponent of MDMA use in the field of psychotherapy. While he is often erroneously credited with the discovery of MDMA, it is the one drug most associated with him. And the one that cost him his DEA drug-handling license. Shulgin is no fan of the irresponsible social use of drugs, but was justifiably outraged by the banning of such a promising therapeutic tool. Such arbitrarily enacted dictates posed the greater threat, Shulgin believed, and voiced his concerns in a letter published in the Journal of Forensic Sciences.

Shulgin took to task the government for passing a law of "carefully worded vagueness" that, in effect, gave control of all medical drug research to the DEA, a law *enforcement* agency – not a law *making* agency. Checks and balances, remember? It certainly seems a good argument. But not one the DEA cared to hear (or wanted anyone else to hear). Not coincidentally, scientific journals began rejecting Shulgin's work. A healthy dose of paranoia moved Shulgin to self-publish his recipes and research, forever placing them in the public domain.

Not long after, the DEA raided Dr. Shulgin's lab. To believe the DEA, Shulgin, after decades of cooperation, copious record keeping and adherence to strict rules, just got sloppy. But what had for years been considered normal chemical storage practices were now deemed "violations." So Shulgin agreed to make his lab more environmentally compliant. The DEA then, shall we say, encouraged Dr. Shulgin to surrender his drug-handling license. Which he did, then got whacked with a reported $25,000 fine. That'll teach him...

But what about the rest of us? What's our lesson? Well, for starters, it seems as though our Founding Fathers' guarantee to life, liberty and the pursuit of happiness has a big fat asterisk behind it. And the fine-print disclaimer defines such inalienably fundamental rights as whatever those in power say they are. Of course parameters make sense. No one wants to see an unbridled human condition on the loose. Or live in a police state. Which is why we have the rule of law, something our Founders cleverly designed to keep everyone honest. At least that was the premise.

Oh, about that surprise I mentioned earlier.

Administrative Law Judge Francis L. Young, while careful not to unduly criticize the DEA for their 1984 evidentiary efforts, found his own lengthy proceedings revealed "much more material about MDMA than the [DEA] Agency was aware of," believing MDMA did in fact have a "currently acceptable medical use."

So, on September 18, 1987, Judge Young ordered the DEA to vacate MDMA from Schedule I. The DEA disagreed and put MDMA back into Schedule I. Really, that's the way it happened. And if you don't believe me, just read Judge Young's 1986 Recommended Decision.

Rule of law, anyone?

NAKED TRUTH VI

Hashish

While marijuana has been on the world's stage for 7,000 years or so, hashish took a bow about 900 AD. Its comparative late arrival could be due to the painstaking manner in which it is produced. The earliest method had workers rub marijuana plants between their palms, slowly collecting the most potent resins until a certain thickness developed and could be scraped away. This they would form into balls, bricks or slabs to be eaten or smoked by aficionados. As an intoxicant, hashish is to marijuana what single malt scotch is to Wild Turkey: same basic stuff but a connoisseur's conceit.

Hashish consumption was then a popular pleasure throughout Persia and Arabia, and soon made its way around the neighborhood. It was not without controversy, even then. Scholarly debates as to the wisdom of its use were held over many decades. Common sense prevailed nearly 500 years before some Ottoman Emir decided otherwise, issuing the first known edict against hashish. It didn't work, of course. Much like today.

One of the more colorful stories regarding hashish has origins in the early 11th century, when a mercenary nutcase by the name of al-Hassan ibn-al-Sabbah recruited followers for the primary purpose of committing assassinations. To get the men in the enlistment mood, al-Hassan purportedly gave them liquid hashish, knocking them out. They awoke in lush, secret gardens, surrounded by beautiful naked women and told it was Paradise. It was all wine, women and song for several blissful hours.

Then it was more liquid hashish and lights out, only to wake back at base camp very disappointed. Was it all a dream? No, said al-Hassan, just a glimpse of Paradise only his powers could provide. And if they wanted more, all they need do was what they were told. Which was to assassinate al-Hassan's enemies or die trying. Either way, it was Paradise on a three-day pass. And the perfect signing bonus. Or so the story goes...

The story also goes that *assassin* and *hashish* are linked as a result. Some say the word assassin derives from the Arabic word haschischin, or hashish user. But being from Persia, al-Hassan and his followers didn't speak Arabic. So in all probability assassin comes from their word Hassassin, meaning disciple of Hassan. Equally probable is that wine was his liquid hammer, as hashish just won't sip – which is not to say they didn't eat it or smoke it on occasion. Anyway, it's just a story. Besides, I've got a better one.

I needed a bit of R&R after my last tango with Murrill Johnson, and there was nothing better than kicking back and watching the Watergate hearings. From first gavel to last, I watched as Sam Ervin and America got the full skinny on Richard Nixon. My take on the finest moment came when Alexander Butterfield gave it up that Mr. Nixon had the Oval Office wired for sound. Right then and there I knew the game was over. I rolled a big fat joint and smoked it down to the nub. Every dog must have its day.

And then came August 9th 1974. That's the day Richard Nixon resigned as president of the United States, boarded Air Force One and headed into rehab. Nixon's addiction was power, possibly the most dangerous drug of all. And not unlike many junkies, he was in denial. Which is why it took the collective intervention of Congress and country to convince Nixon to get clean, if not come clean. (Debate continues as to whether either actually occurred, but my money says he died dirty.) I stayed high for three months.

And then I joined the Army, which is where the story really starts. I wanted to go to Europe, but had all of about 20 bucks to my name. The Army presented a good way to get there and stay awhile, so I took their offer. Plus, I figured a little duty and honor on my resume of life couldn't hurt. Patriotism may very well be the last refuge to which a scoundrel seeks, but I liked the GI Bill too.

It was a restless world back then – parts of it believed Nixon got the boot for bungling Vietnam – and our military was, understandably, more than a little concerned. A real fear was that the Soviets might make a move, test us somewhere. Maybe even come through East Berlin with their particular version of reunification. So the military snapped to, none more briskly than our nuclear missile sites.

My deal with the Army said I could pick any job in exchange for them sending me anywhere needed in what was then West Germany. I picked Quartermaster Corps, mainly because movies and *M*A*S*H* made working supply look pretty smart. And I was hoping the Army needed me someplace cool, like Munich. But my final destination was a nuclear missile site in the remote western countryside. Barely 100 soldiers strong and all male, our unit didn't even qualify as a fort. We were designated a "line battery." And it wasn't long before all I could think about was the caveat to be careful what you wish for.

During the Vietnam pullout, our battery was often used as a way station for returning soldiers too close to discharge for permanent assignment elsewhere. Military discipline and decorum went AWOL, and the place was an absolute zoo. It had failed Inspector General reviews for two years running and been chewing up commanding officers left and right, with the last spit out several months prior. I reported to a master sergeant just marking time, awaiting the new zookeeper.

Captain Freddie G. Wilson got that call, assuming command shortly after my arrival. He'd come up through the enlisted ranks to fly choppers in Vietnam, and been promised the rank of major if he could transform our unit into something resembling regular Army. It would be his last tour of duty and one he wanted to make a success, as the pension for a retiring major was significantly better than that of a captain. But a quick look around and he was having thoughts similar to mine.

Interviewing all battery personnel holding positions of authority was first on Captain Wilson's list. Technically, my sergeant ran the supply room. He was an affable lifer but a functional illiterate, so Captain Wilson called me in. He made it known he wasn't much for college boys, but nonetheless appreciated the fact I agreed with his assessment of conditions – a shared misery we both looked to rectify. And it didn't hurt I had been the recipient of the Army's American Spirit Honor Medal for leadership. Anyway, it was his longest interview.

He asked what I believed would best whip our little cast of characters into a cohesive military unit, at least long enough to pass the next Inspector General review. The fact we were out of Vietnam, I told him, was a good start. So was having a recent combat officer in charge. Discipline would improve, even if only slightly at first. He agreed. And we both agreed chronic substance abuse posed our biggest security risk. Where we disagreed, though, was how best to crack the whip.

Captain Wilson was all for zero tolerance. He had seen enough drugs in Vietnam. His position was drug-test everyone and let the chips fall where they may. Except that when the chips fell, I explained, there would hardly be anyone left to pick them up, including me. And he could forget the upcoming Inspector General review, not to mention that gold cluster insignia of major he wanted so bad he could taste it. So I proposed a more pragmatic approach, one that would focus on the worst substance abusers. There weren't many, and their quick disposal presented him the opportunity to establish firmer control – and a smart way to starch the shorts of everyone else.

Because it was everyone else that was going to carry the captain's water. And everyone else used one substance or another to fight the creeping psychosis of being stationed out in the middle of nowhere, sitting atop a bevy of nuclear missiles aimed east toward Armageddon. No one was exempt. Hell, even the captain confessed a medicinal drink or two and sometimes three, but always remained on top of his game. Convincing him recreational drug users were capable of playing the same game wasn't easy that day, but it came to form the premise of our Faustian collaboration.

Alcohol was the drug abuse of choice. Those who mainly drank alone and barely went through the motions of soldiering were tagged for transfer. So were the hardened heroin and amphetamine addicts, for their performance was just as dismal. All of which happened at double-time, leaving everyone else of every stripe wearing starched shorts and pretty much eyes wide open. And I outranked all but a handful.

Rank may have its privilege in the Army, but positions of power – especially at remote installations – tend to trump it (our mail clerk was a god). By being the de facto head of supply, where every requisition from toilet paper to nuclear warheads required my signature, I presented Captain Wilson a twofer: rank and power. But it took critical and calculated benevolence by the captain to get a firm hand on the recreational drug used by nearly 90% of all remaining battery personnel: hashish.

So it was with Captain Wilson's knowledge and tacit approval that I brought discipline to the business of hashish at our little nuclear hideout. I monopolized it simply by not being greedy – and selling better hashish. I also sold the deal, which was to pass the next Inspector General review. Work smart and sober and show some GI Joe, and the captain would cast a blind eye. Work stupid and stoned and all bets were off. It was a good deal. Most guys bought it.

Captain Wilson kept his end of the bargain, earning the respect of the men. He had mine, even before allowing me to keep my investment capital in his office safe. But let's not forget, it was still a nuclear missile site. And manned by soldiers that, by and large, were smoking hashish the rest of the time. As horrifying as that seems, and at times it was, it wasn't drug-induced befuddlement that precipitated the most frightening incident during my nuclear days. Nope, that came at the hands of one stone-cold sober first lieutenant.

Soldiers who manned the guard towers surrounding the launch site downrange had the worst jobs. It was lonely, sitting solo high above the nukes, but mission critical. It was twelve hours on, twelve hours off. But shift trades meant some soldiers pulled double, even triple duty. And just about every one of them took amphetamines. It wasn't always pretty, but they did stay focused – just like little Johnny on Ritalin in sixth grade.

More bored than hopped-up one night, two guards decided to squeeze off a couple of rounds at the other's perch, seeing who could come the closest without scoring a direct hit. (The first few rounds in all our clips were tracer bullets, glowing trajectories easily determining the winning shot.) Like I said, it wasn't always pretty. Anyway, it was incredibly stupid and dangerous behavior. But so was the punishment.

Captain Wilson was away, leaving the downrange lieutenant in command when the shots were fired: think Barney Fife during a Mayberry bank robbery with sheriff Taylor up in Raleigh. Using one-bullet logic, our young lieutenant decides to teach all a lesson and locks down all the ammunition, leaving our nuclear missile site literally defenseless for nearly 24 hours. I am not kidding. And this was when terrorist organizations such as the Bader-Meinhoff Gang and The Red Army Faction were in close proximity and looking for any weakness. Don't even try to imagine. It took a long time for that to become funny.

Gimme today's Army anytime, folks. And I'm sure Freddie Wilson would agree. But we had to play the hand dealt. Not all the cards were outright winners, but teamwork and trust saved the day. We passed the next Inspector General review. And America slept better. Freddie G. Wilson was one hell of a man and should've been a general, but was not passed over for major.

And I passed my free time high on hashish and riding trains. I visited great museums. Saw beautiful architecture. Took-in my first nude beach and watched Little Feat give the Rolling Stones a run for their money in Stuttgart. Heard Eric Burton sing a drunken yet truly inspired House of the Rising Sun under a small tent in the rain, somewhere. Met very interesting frauleins; one a fencing champion, another a beautiful, junkie nurse. I flirted with all the old ladies running the local bakeries. Every taxi was a Mercedes Benz. And Camels were twenty cents a pack at the PX. Who couldn't have a good time?

My only real complaint was not being allowed to remain stateside with family when my father died in March of 1976. But that was a small thing, as dad and I finally reconciled after my receiving the American Spirit Honor Medal. Standing at that podium, giving my speech, and seeing my father seated with generals and beaming was an exceptional moment, one undiminished after all these years.

Ain't life funny...

What lacks any and all humor, though, is that hashish remains on Schedule I of the Controlled Substance Act and possession is still a felony in the United States. Someone will go to jail for it today and tomorrow, and that is a legislative travesty. And if hashish were truly an assassin's accessory, then just about everyone in Amsterdam should be dead by now. But they're not. And smoking parlors there are about as common as 7-Elevens here.

Amsterdam has taken an enlightened approach to marijuana and hashish use. They determined, and are currently demonstrating, laws against cannabis consumption simply do not work. And their only real drug problem is with cocaine and heroin — both of which are generally avoided by hashish and marijuana smokers there, ripping a big hole in the hot-air balloon floated here that marijuana is a gateway drug.

Amsterdam is a city full of history, inspiring works of art and wonderful architecture, even if some of it leans funny. It was the last stop on my recent travels, shortly after my visit with the distinguished Albert Hofmann. And it seemed the perfect place to reflect on such a rewarding experience. I smoked the world's best hashish over four fine days, spending just $40 — a mere pittance to the king's ransom I'd pay for the same pleasure here in the United States.

And that pleasure should be mine, and yours if you want it. It won't make you crazy, yet it just might make Cosmos and other cocktails a little passé. Which is what has the alcohol industry smiling through clenched teeth. But sleep tight, boys. Remember: you beat all those Turkish smoking parlors of yesteryear in a fair fight. And rest assured you'll do it again. Legalization will end your long monopoly on intoxicants, but then a little competition is a good thing.

Right?

NAKED TRUTH VII

Opium

Someone coined the phrase "the only constant is change." It's a good one, applicable almost across the board. But someone else coined the corollary phrase "some things never change." Also a good one, and one I've chosen to describe opium use. Because the first known written reference; by the Sumerians of southwest Asia around 6,000 years ago, describes the poppy flower, whose gummy extract is opium, as *hul gil* – plant of joy. Like I said, some things never change.

From the time of those ancient Sumerians forward, opium use has continued a part of recorded history. Sculpture of the Roman god of sleep, Somnos, was adorned with poppies – placing the origins of "flower power" well before the 60s. Poppies can be found in Egyptian pictography, illustrating their priests/physicians as using an opium remedy called "thebacium" (named after potent poppies grown near their capital city of Thebes). Dug-up dead Pharaohs were found with opium artifacts within reach, just in case the afterlife got a little boring.

Homer wrote about opium in *The Odyssey,* speaking of Telemachus and his grief over not finding his father, Odysseus. Helen slipped the depressed Telemachus a cocktail of wine and opium, described by Homer as a potion "that had the power of robbing grief and anger of their sting and banishing all painful memories." And had more professors highlighted that aspect of *The Odyssey,* fewer college students would have taken the Cliff's Notes shortcut.

Ancient Greek physicians, most notably Galen, would grind the whole poppy plant or use its opium extract to remedy nearly every known malady from persistent headaches and melancholy to "the trouble to which women are subject." Galen may have been the earliest snake oil salesman (a little opium for your PMS, my dear?), but later physicians were no less enthusiastic. Opium was variously referred to as the Sacred Anchor of Life, Milk of Paradise, Destroyer of Grief and the Hand of God.

That invocation of God's purpose for the poppy was heralded in the 14th century by a fellow named Paracelsus, a German-Swiss doctor, who wrote, "I possess a secret remedy which I call *laudanum* [literally, "something to be praised"] and which is superior to all other heroic remedies." Then the physician Thomas Sydenham, a 17th century maven of English medicine, proclaimed that "among the remedies which it has pleased Almighty God to give to man to relieve his sufferings, none is so universal and so efficacious as opium."

Opium enjoyed its exalted status for more than 5,000 years, mostly as a medicine but also as social recreation, reinforcing the notion that the line between pleasure and pain is a fine one indeed. It was physician Sydenham that standardized Paracelsus' *laudanum* brew, taking two ounces of opium, an ounce of saffron with a pinch of cinnamon and cloves, all shaken and probably stirred inside a pint of cheap wine. Bingo, laudanum was a hit. British imports of opium skyrocketed to around 300,000 pounds by 1860.

The British Empire, through The British East India Company, wielded a monopoly over India's opium production and its worldwide distribution, but preferred Turkish opium for her subjects. Why? Because Turkish opium was the better buzz, that's why. Those kinky Brits... Anyway, buying laudanum and raw opium in 19th century England was easy and acceptable, available at pharmacies and even grocery stores.

A century before Ritalin, English parents were encouraged to medicate their colicky children with concoctions known to contain opium. Cute names like *Godfrey's Cordial, Street's Infants Quietness* and, my favorite, *Mrs. Winslow's Soothing Syrup*, made the whole thing wholesome. And you can bet whoever Mrs. Winslow was had a little laudanum at the ready for rainy days. It was as British as fish and chips.

More than a few British writers developed an affinity for opium. Before putting pen to paper to write his masterpiece *Kubla Khan,* Samuel Taylor Coleridge (1772-1834) first primed his creative side with big-boy doses of opium. Another fellow Brit and writer, Thomas de Quincey, waxes poetically of opium's superiority over alcohol in *Confessions of an English Opium-Eater* (1821): "Wine constantly leads a man to the brink of absurdity and extravagance, and, beyond a certain point, it is sure to volatilize and disperse the intellectual energies; whereas opium seems to compose what has been agitated, and to concentrate what has been distracted."

Conventional wisdom in de Quincey's time held that opium users were dullards who squandered life's opportunities – junk science easily debunked by de Quincey. He had a recognized intellect, and loved the opera: often he attended under the dreamy influence of opium, finding the experience exquisite. To wit: "Now opium, by greatly increasing the activity of the mind, generally increases, of necessity, that particular mode of its activity by which we are able to construct out of the raw material of organic sound an elaborate intellectual pleasure." Hmmm…got opium?

That British East India Company, the one with the worldwide opium monopoly, got into an absolute stink over it with China around 1839, precipitating the first of two Opium Wars. The Opium Wars had numerous instigations, but the catalyst was China's refusal to legalize opium for her people. Now, it's not like China was new to opium. Opium and its uses first appeared in Chinese texts dating back to the 12th century. So there were no virgins.

No, the bone of contention was restraint of trade. China wasn't crazy about opium, but she was deathly afraid of throwing open her doors to the wild and woolly West. A self-sufficient people, believing China the "Heavenly Middle Kingdom," they viewed all Westerners, especially the British, as "barbarians." Not ignorant to the outside world, China had seen neighbors fall to colonialism, some to total domination.

Reason enough, the Chinese argued, to keep the barbarians at bay. What trade China allowed was tightly controlled. To which the British objected and went to war. Twice. In the resulting uneven spoils of war, opium – and open trade – were forced upon China and the British Empire took Hong Kong, keeping it nearly 150 years.

But it wasn't just the British. Across the Atlantic existed a parallel fascination with opium. We had our British East India Trading Company wannabe in the guise of New Yorker John Jacob Astor, whose American Fur Company purchased then sold tons of Turkish opium to China. For every de Quincey we had a William Blair. And we gave opium concoctions like *Ayer's Sarsaparilla* to our sickly children at a time when patent medicines were more readily accessible than medical practitioners.

By 1875, America was an industrialized nation of 39 states inhabited by a growing population, many newly arriving immigrants. Though not always as welcome as "give me your tired, your poor…" seemed to suggest, many flourished. Many did not, none less so than the Chinese. Schooners and steamers brought them to San Francisco, glad to take the backbreaking railroad jobs connecting East to West. And we gave them nothing but a hard time in return.

Laws against wearing ponytails – the traditional Chinese style – were quickly passed. Other harassments, some as silly as how water could be carried, also came to be. There were regulations against certain types of laundries, mostly owned by Chinese, running many out of business. Most damaging were local newspaper editorials, lurid accounts warning opium made women crazy horny, and that all sorts of drug-induced debauchery occurred inside opium dens. Within a year, in 1876, a law passed banning the smoking of opium in San Francisco's Chinatown.

But if you lived anywhere else in America, opium consumption remained legal. And you could buy it mail order from the pages of Sears and Roebuck's catalog. Raw opium and its derivatives, like laudanum, were prominently advertised and cheaper than beer – and quite popular with women. The virtuous ones avoided booze and bars, preferring to congregate in parlors and on porches and take their pause with laudanum tinctures. (And while editors exaggerated the crazy horny part, being a mailman was probably a good job.)

Opiates remained popular medicinal and recreational tonics in the United States until the aftermath of the Spanish-American War. Said to stem from a dispute over Cuba and Puerto Rico, it was settled in 1898. And when the spoils were divvied up, America claimed, among other things, the Philippine Islands. Though a mostly Catholic people, there were some Muslims and a few pagans and even fewer Episcopalians. So the Episcopalian church appointed Charles Henry Brent their first Missionary Bishop to the Philippines.

Not content just bringing the Word to those Filipino heathens (especially the Catholic ones), Bishop Brent fancied himself a drug czar and set about against the opium trade. That he largely failed should come as no surprise, given the historical realities of opium consumption. Another failure, but one the bishop thought a success, was coordinating the first worldwide crusade against opiates.

To save his new sheep from the opium wolf, Bishop Brent knew China was key. It was from there the opium flowed. Praying mightily for guidance no doubt, the best the bishop could divine was a plea to the U.S. government for help, lending some doubt as to whether his prayers were actually answered. Anyway, Brent sends word to president Teddy Roosevelt, imploring him and America to lead an international drug convention to control, if not eradicate, China's opium trade.

President Roosevelt had great ambitions for 20th century America. We were flexing our muscles and morals both home and abroad, and ready to challenge Great Britain as the world's commercial power. And China was the playing field. That China was asking for our help with opium gave Roosevelt his in. He saw Bishop Brent's international drug convention as merely a humanitarian means to an economic end, and quickly agreed. In questionable good faith, Congress passed the first federal ban on opium importation.

The International Opium Commission was the fruit of Bishop Brent's labor, convening February 1, 1909 in Shanghai. The good bishop was front and center as our delegation head, preaching to the assembled on the immoral evils of opium. One short-term success was the dismantling of the India-China opium trade route. Short-term because, like squeezing a balloon, it popped up immediately elsewhere. Chinese demand continued and was easily met, exposing the fly in Bishop Brent's opium ointment, not to mention spreading a few nails across America's moral high road taken to China's market.

Meanwhile, back at the ranch, we're consuming opiates like nobody's business and had been for decades, all perfectly legal. While lives were certainly put to ruin, society suffered little associated crime. Not when the next fix was cheap and as close as Sears. But that was against God's will, something Bishop Brent convinced the world. And what had once been revered as the Hand of God was now reviled as a Tool of the Devil. God save us all...

And start with me, I guess. Because I find opium every bit the pleasure de Quincy did. My affection began back in my nuclear missile days, in fact, the very first morning. I was on the bus to Kaiserslautern, heading toward a boring day of final processing-in, seated next to the soldier I replaced. He was off to the airport and home and been high for days. Though useless for any insights into the job, he did offer me a pea-size piece of raw opium. He told me to eat it, saying it would make things more interesting. And it did.

None more so than my security clearance interview. It was very thorough, given my assignment to a nuclear missile site. The process lasted an hour, part of which was a tutorial on the difficulties surrounding my assignment, given the mess it was in. At its conclusion, the conducting officer took me aside and commended my professionalism, saying I was just what the Army needed. I was educated, mature, a serious soldier. Of course, I lied about taking drugs, but I figured if he couldn't tell, I sure wasn't going to. And besides, I considered myself a serious soldier. Anyway, I didn't see opium again for months.

When I did, I bought the equivalent of six or seven pea-size pieces, a small supply lasting a full year. I ate some but preferred smoking, always discreet, usually on a 3-day pass somewhere having fun, where common sense kept me from having too much fun. And in a legal environment, you could expect my conduct, as well as likeminded others, to be guided by the same principles. And the rest, well, there are idiots in every group. But the responsible use theory will work, just as it does for alcohol, and we've got more than a few idiots in that group, don't we?

Since those Army days, I have had the occasion to enjoy opium only a handful of times. And what I've learned is that a little opium goes a long way: occasional and short duration use will cause few problems for society, produce minimal habituation and nary a criminal. While it is doubtful Sears would desire to be in the opium business today, someone needs to be.

And not just because I like opium, but because the world does. It has for many centuries, despite all good and bad attempts to alter that simple truth. The horse is long dead; so let's quit beating it – and each other for the frailty of our human condition. Just stop it. Stop it from all church and bully pulpits. Accept those among us who will do no harm, and be humane in our care of those who harm only themselves. It is the only way.

Because some things never change.

NAKED TRUTH VIIa
Morphine

Man, being the curious beast, often gets more than bargained for. One such man was German pharmacist Friedrich Saturner. Opium was widely used as both medicinal and recreational tonics by the 19th century, but Saturner focused on the medicinal value, seeking a way to intensify its painkilling properties. Around 1803, Saturner found that by dissolving opium in acid, and then neutralizing the result with ammonia, he produced an alkaloid ten times the strength of raw opium. After sampling his creation, he named it morphine – after Morpheus, the god of dreams.

Morphine was a hit, quickly becoming a staple inside every doctor's little black bag. And in a testament to their fundamental ignorance regarding addiction, many physicians believed it a non-addictive cure for alcoholism. Yet even as that theory proved very wrong, morphine remained popular with those treating the disease: the new theory being an opiate habitué was preferable to an alcoholic. Morphine users were sedate by definition, more often solitary in their practice and few, if any, beat the wife and kids – or each other.

Say what you want about that theory, but morphine proved its weight in gold as a painkiller. Administered orally, or directly to the wound, it revolutionized surgery at a time when a good doctor was a fast doctor. Amputation was common and performed on the wide-awake. As good as morphine was, it took another curious fellow designing the first syringe, allowing the drug to reach its full potential. That was in 1843, when Dr. Alexander Wood sought a better route of drug administration. He discovered the effects of morphine, when injected intravenously, were instantaneous and far more potent than oral dosing.

And just in time for the Civil War. Battlefield doctors used butcher knives, saws and wire-cutters to hack and snap away any limb with a bullet hole, a hard task made harder working around five or six soldiers restraining the screaming patient. Imagine being that first surgeon to amputate an arm or leg of a soldier made calm by a syringe full of morphine. Imagine your prayers being answered. Just imagine what you would call this miracle. Well, those battlefield docs called it GOM – God's Own Medicine. And tens of thousands of Civil War amputees agreed.

But not for long. While the Civil War settled things, sort of, it created a generation of men addicted to morphine. Doctors came up with a name for that too. They called it the Army's Disease. Morphine was certainly not the cure, but it was all a crippled man had to ease the pain – and the painful memories. So we gave it to them, all the while selling it to everyone else for $1.50: the Sears catalog price for a syringe, two needles and two vials of morphine, all delivered in a shiny carrying case.

The times they were a changin', though. Bishop Brent and other religious leaders in cahoots with temperance crusaders preached not only the immorality of opiates, they condemned users as immoral. Those who took opiates were judged as weak, a pox on society and acting against God's will. And while the prospect of eternal damnation would seem dire consequence enough, a little hell on earth couldn't hurt.

There was no clear idea in the early 1900s just how many Americans were habituated to opiates, save the surviving Civil War amputees, and even they were hard to quantify. But moral indignation was not. And it was getting louder. There existed a genuine fear opiates were enslaving America, but when the fear of God was not enough to ensure emancipation, Bishop Brent beseeched – some say blackmailed – the government to do his bidding.

Which didn't happen overnight. Bishop Brent's international opium conference took ten years to plan and didn't convene until 1909. It would take another six years before passage of the Harrison Narcotics Act placed "illegal possession" into the American lexicon. The law required those in the business of dispensing opiates – doctors, pharmacists and even Sears – to be licensed and, of course, pay a tax. (Revenue issues were the ruse around our pesky constitutional rights.) Everyone else was going to jail.

Which ended up being mostly doctors. That's right, doctors. Within five years, more than 10,000 had been handcuffed and hauled away in paddy wagons. Some were dose-happy and irresponsible, but the many were humane practitioners caught between doing what they saw as right and what the law said was wrong. Physicians considered opiate habituation a disease producing far less societal misery than alcoholism. And given their druthers, many doctors considered opiate habitués the better lot.

But not being given their druthers is what upset doctors most. Specifically, they took the Harrison Narcotics Act to task for decreeing opiates could only be prescribed in the due course of medical treatment, which they believed gave government a chair inside the examining room, deciding who was sick and who wasn't. And the government decided if you took opiates just to make it through the night, or day, you weren't sick at all – just a menace.

The Harrison Narcotics Act of 1914 was one of America's most ambitious experiments in social engineering since claiming Independence in 1776. By 1923 half of all inmates in Leavenworth penitentiary were federal drug offenders. At least the level of their health care was good, what with all those doctors in the next cell. But the experiment failed America. In terms of population percentages, opiate habituation has changed little in the near 90 years since Harrison became law.

So, where would we be had the Harrison Narcotics Act never happened? Would we be the nation of immoral morphine addicts prophesied by the likes of Bishop Brent and William Randolph Hearst? Not on a bet. Before Harrison, remember, morphine was unregulated and abundant. Anyone could be an addict if so inclined. Yet the disinclined comprised nearly 98% of the population: an absolute epidemic of responsible people. And about the same number we can expect with the repeal of prohibition.

So it's a pretty good bet that had Harrison never happened, and all things considered, things would have largely remained the same. Doctors and druggists would still be in control, and doing a better job. Society's addicts no longer able to maintain functional lives would be treated humanely, removed from harm's way, if not their own. And I could cozy up with a little opium now and then. And the hundreds of billions of dollars squandered these last hundred years trying to stop us would have made certain fiscal quandaries today less so. Social Security, Medicare, Iraq – quandaries like that.

Knowing what we know now, which is more than they knew then, how many of you would give legal morphine a whirl? That's what I thought. And I'm with you. Morphine is not a recreational drug. Shoot morphine for a few days and you'll be shooting it every day and know, without a doubt, you're an addict. You may lie to yourself for a while, but not for long. And you may live a functional life, just not a long one. There are few old addicts.

And while mankind's penchant for opiates has been known for six millenniums, it wasn't until the early 1970s that we knew why: it appears the human body is actually built for the stuff. Using a relatively new process of radioactive tracers, neuroscientists at Johns Hopkins University were able to track the neural pathways opiates followed in the brain. This led to the discovery of opiate receptors, something all God's children possess: something squarely at odds with Bishop Brent's contention opium use was against God's plan. Go figure.

The first time black market morphine crossed my path I passed. The second time too. And when I see it again, I'll do the same. But there are times when I wouldn't mind making more kidney stones. My first bout sent me to the emergency room where, once the crew concluded I wasn't scamming for drugs, they injected me with morphine. Within seconds the pain left, leaving me thinking maybe these kidney stones had merit. I was certain somewhere around that fifth injection in the ensuing pre-surgery hours. The god of dreams, indeed...

But the nightmares are real, too. Just ask Friedrich Saturner. Though the world owes him great debt, the price he paid, that part not bargained, was watching his wife die of a morphine overdose. While not much is known of Mrs. Saturner's mental state, leaving open the case for either accident or anguish, her death nonetheless tells a cautionary tale, underscoring the precision of morphine, and its seduction.

But enough of all that – let's talk about Rush Limbaugh.

NAKED TRUTH VIIb
Thebaine

An alkaloid of opium, thebaine is semi-synthetic morphine, used in the manufacturing of painkilling drugs such as oxycodone and hydrocodone, pills more commonly known to us, respectively, as Oxycotin and Vicodin. They provide the same plusses and minuses of morphine but without the needle – and are Rush Limbaugh's drugs of choice.

Rush Limbaugh is very adept at pushing society's buttons and, depending on whether your politics lean left or right, is an idiot or an inspiration. But that's not the point. The point is this: if opiate consumption were an Olympic event, Rush Limbaugh would easily take the gold and dramatically raise the bar. The man could pop some pills, folks.

And it seems he did so every day for several years, all the while giving no indication his wittiness and musings stemmed and flowed from a brain soaked in opiates. What a wonderful display. And while he may not get away with it completely, as the law does apply, he seems no worse for wear. But it's early yet, so stay tuned. In the meantime, he's back on the air for ditto-heads and detractors alike. Which begs the question I've yet to hear asked.

Did any of it make any difference?

Rush stills sounds like Rush. Of course, his morphine monkey whispers differently now. So I'm thinking had Rush been able to obtain his opiates over the counter instead of under some table, he'd still be doing them today. And anyone who doesn't believe that should go stand in the corner with those who think it mere coincidence Rush came clean just as the Feds came knocking.

But you can't blame him, not really. And I'm even willing to defend the man. Rush should be able to do opiates to his heart's content and without fear, other than having his bowel movements chronicled by a few Xs on a whole calendar of pages. Because opiates will bind you tight: just taking the normal prescription of 20 Vicodin over the course of a week can strain such things considerably. That Rush consumed the equivalent of one prescription every day for years is where any and all sympathies should lie, and punishment enough. Think about it, but don't dwell.

Let's move on. While I believe consuming raw opium the better choice, it lacks the anonymity and, more to the point, access pharmaceutical opiates provide. Our taking so many pills for so many things lends commonality to the practice, allowing it to hide in plain sight. And finding so many pills to take is easy, if not fraught with risk, as demonstrated by Rush Limbaugh.

Such off-label use of oxycodone and hydrocodone is not nearly as chronic as we are led to believe, and society's dangers are overblown. This is not to say opiates are safe, of course, just that the overwhelming majority consumed are done so safely. Deaths have occurred, but autopsies reveal a cornucopia of co-conspirator drugs, usually alcohol and other potent painkillers, including heroin. Which seems to suggest long-standing drug addicts, and not recreational users, are at the greatest risk.

Now, I'm no Rush Limbaugh. But, like him, my introduction to hydrocodone was the result of great pain – a blown disc in my lower vertebrae. My doctor had me on 10mg Vicodin, and I was eating them like candy. And during the three weeks leading up to my surgery, I consumed nearly a hundred. After the surgery, I took about as many. And when I quit, I suffered no real withdrawals. I did, however, discover the indelicate side effects of extended opiate consumption.

That was 1998. My back still talks to me every day. Mostly it's just a whisper and little distraction. But the four or five times a year when it does get my attention, I don't want more needles inserted near my spine, emitting electrical impulses to trick my brain – one of the more esoteric procedures in pain management I've experienced. No, give me a few Vicodin for a few days and I'm happy. The pain goes away, even muting the whisper, while bringing a certain pleasure. A pleasure I occasionally enjoy without the pain, if you know what I mean. And many of you do.

But do you feel like a criminal? Of course not. But get caught with a few Vicodin in your purse and you will. It's those mug shots and fingerprints. And though you could actually go to jail, most small-quantity first offenders are ordered to participate in a drug awareness program. Some programs make you call every day, and if your number or color comes up, you must immediately report for testing. Others are just as intrusive. All are a waste of time and money. They deter the habitual user only for the term of the program, and leave the others mad as hell.

And none of us should take it anymore.

NAKED TRUTH VIII

Heroin

Heroin. You don't even need to say the word out loud. Just reading it conjures up the image of a bicep tied-off with a rubber tube, a bulging vein at the elbow cradle punctured by a needle, all in close-up and bad lighting. Right? That's the way it is. But that's not the way it was. While morphine revolutionized medicine, society at large was misled, albeit unintentionally. Once morphine's dark side was discovered, a worldwide search began to find a non-addictive, yet just as effective, alternative.

An Englishman named C. R. Wright was one of many searchers. Boiling morphine over a stove one day in 1874, Wright produced the first rough draft of heroin. But for reasons not entirely known, Wright's efforts were put to little use. Then, around 1895, German Heinrich Dreser, a scientist for the Bayer Company (the aspirin folks), diluted morphine with acetyls and created diacetylmorphine. Alluding

129

to its heroic properties, Bayer trademarks the substance heroin. And the world changed.

Heroin was marketed as a non-addictive cure for respiratory diseases like pneumonia and tuberculosis, both common and often killers at the dawn of the 20th century. It was an instant hit, replacing morphine in medical bags and medicine chests. But it wasn't just respiratory diseases on heroin's hit list: Bayer put alcoholics and morphine addicts in the crosshairs. Many doctors agreed, and, once again, a trusting public signed-on.

So did the Saint James Society, a faith-based ministry of good works praying for God's help in recapturing souls considered lost to morphine. Apparently, God told them heroin was the answer. In the early 1900s they ran a busy mail-order operation, sending free heroin to any morphine habitué desiring redemption – or on a tight budget. So now I'm confused. Because while all this is going on, Bishop Brent is also hearing from God. And God is telling him opiates are a definite no-no, which makes me wonder. Does God have *that* kind of a sense of humor? Or is it maybe all those voices they were hearing were just voices?

No matter. Heroin was here to stay. Switching from morphine had a learning curve for addict dose amounts, as heroin was the more powerful drug, requiring less. And while it may be debatable shooting morphine is better than shooting heroin, not much really changed for the addict. Many continued living productive lives, though often in quiet desperation, something the moralists deemed not punishment enough, demanding in the name of God something more be done.

It is important to note that the number of American addicts remained stable after heroin was introduced. Most were morphine addicts to begin with, or alcoholics. For them it was just trading one drug for another and another promise broken. For as early as 1902 doctors discovered heroin to be even more addictive than morphine. Which explains why the overwhelming majority of Americans shunned both. But again, that wasn't good enough for the moralists.

And one of the most vocal and influential moralists of the time was William Jennings Bryan. He became a lawyer and then a politician: Nebraskans elected him to Congress in 1890 and sent him back in 1892. He never won another election, losing a Senate race in 1894 and three times as the Democrat's presidential nominee, the last in 1908. But he remained a powerful voice within the Democratic Party, variously as a newspaper editor and publisher and speech-maker, and then secretary of state for Woodrow Wilson.

When World War I erupted in Europe, Bryan was at odds with Wilson, advocating strict neutrality. Things came to a head when German submarines sank the British passenger ship RMS Lusitania, killing 1,198 on board, including 128 Americans. Believing Wilson would use the incident to enter the war – and "Remember the Lusitania!" on U.S. recruitment posters seems to suggest he did – Bryan resigns as secretary of state. With his political influence waning, he turns even more to evangelism.

Bryan preached the consumption of alcohol immoral, and became a leading crusader for passage of our 18th Amendment, ushering the carnage of Prohibition to center stage. But the biggest thorn in Bryan's side was Darwin and his theory of evolution. As a literal interpreter of Scriptures, Bryan believed in Adam and Eve, not Darwin's monkey. Bryan barnstormed America, demanding states pass anti-evolution laws. Several did, including Tennessee, passing

131

the Butler Law, which set the stage for Bryan's most famous fifteen minutes, the Scopes trial of 1925 – more commonly known as the "Monkey Trial."

John T. Scopes was a young Tennessee teacher of high school biology and, like every other science teacher, used the textbook "Civic Biology," which taught evolution. To test Tennessee's new law and, by their own admission, discredit Bryan, ACLU legal beagles schemed to have Scopes arrested. The infamous Clarence Darrow joined the fight, proclaiming that for years "I've wanted to put Bryan in his place as a bigot." Bryan saw the trial as a "contest between evolution and Christianity...a duel to the death," and labeled Darrow "the greatest atheist or agnostic in the United States." Scopes who?

Anyway, public sentiment was on Bryan's side. It wasn't until Darrow, thwarted in all attempts to introduce testimony by pro-evolution scholars, put Bryan on the witness stand that public sentiment changed. In what many call a brilliant cross-examination, Darrow humiliated Byran, succeeding in exposing him as a bigot, if not deranged. Darrow lost the case as planned (wanting to test the constitutionally of Butler on appeal, which, due to a technicality regarding Scope's $100 fine, couldn't happen), and Bryan got his "duel to the death," dying a broken man several days later.

So, you ask, what does all that have to do with drugs? Well, William Jennings Bryan, while secretary of state, was the man behind the man introducing the Harrison Narcotics Act of 1914. (And had we the courage and foresight to stop such a travesty, putting Bryan in his place then instead of later, a good case can be made Prohibition would never have seen the light of day.) Bryan was the secular twin to

Bishop Brent, with both claiming to hear God's voice. Almost makes you wish God were a mute.

Or, at least, that we would have listened more to doctors. Many quickly concluded heroin an unnecessary redundancy, citing morphine more than enough to manage the disease of addiction and urged heroin be banned. Had they succeeded, and Brent and Bryan failed, America, if not the world, could have put the heroin genie back inside the bottle. Instead, Harrison subordinated medicine to the moralists. And ten thousand doctors went to jail.

But not all went quietly. One such physician, a Dr. Webb, appealed his conviction all the way to the Supreme Court. It seems Webb, who had duly registered under Harrison and paid the requisite tax, believed drug addiction a disease. And a druggist named Goldbaum, also a registered taxpayer, agreed. Dr. Webb wrote his patients morphine prescriptions and Goldbaum filled them, something the Feds considered a maintenance conspiracy and not a good faith attempt at cure. The Court heard the case January 16, 1919.

WEBB, et al. v. United States, 249 U.S. 96, was decided March 3, 1919. In a decision arguably more important than that of the 2000 presidential election, the Supreme Court split 5 to 4 in favor of Harrison, and, by uncomfortable extension, Bryan and Brent. That was it. That date, March 3, 1919, should resonate in our history as another day of infamy. For it was that day America's drug war really began, the day of the fool's errand, the day moralists hearing voices silenced all voice of reason. March 3, 1919.

By then it was all over but the shouting. Doctors and druggist by the thousands had been arrested, and the rest had been effectively cowed. And a black market in heroin was thriving, forcing opiate habitués to deal with unprincipled drug dealers instead of doctors. Sears too was forced to quit the drug business, generating, no doubt, a softer bottom line and a little ill will in the corporate boardroom.

But the doctors had it right. And it wasn't like they didn't warn us, either. On May 15, 1915, just weeks after Harrison's effective date, an editorial published in the respected New York Medical Journal stated: "The really serious results of this legislation, however, will only appear gradually and will not always be recognized as such. These will be the failures of promising careers, the disrupting of happy families, the commission of crimes which will never be traced to their real cause, and the influx into hospitals to the mentally disordered of many who would otherwise live socially competent lives." Right as rain.

They were right about addiction, too. Addiction to any substance, whether to alcohol or tobacco, opiates or crack, is a disease. And until medical science finds what in our DNA triggers the sickness, society must treat all so afflicted no less humanely than patients suffering other genetic dysfunction. Or at the very least treat them like our alcoholics, and trust in your heart there will be a whole lot less of them, not to mention an end to a 90-year crime wave.

And then came Prohibition. Booze was illegal, so were drugs and prostitution: a virtual trifecta in the vice game for crime bosses. Lucky Luciano masterminded the heroin smuggling ring immortalized in the Hollywood movie *French Connection*, importing from Marseilles nearly all America's heroin. For decades the mob owned the marketplace. It didn't really grow much, mind you, but it didn't need to. Heroin prices skyrocketed and profits were enormous. And it's a coin toss who suffered more, society or the addict.

But we do know how long the suffering has gone on, and it is time we end it. It is time we quit listening to those voices. Ninety years is long enough. And while the thought of drugs being regulated and obtainable without prescription gives many of us more than a little pause, imagine instead the breathtaking reduction in street crime. Some estimate it at nearly 80%, and not just because they're cock-eyed optimists. Government statistics back them up.

The Justice Department contends almost eight out of ten personal and property crimes committed are by addicts to pay inflated prices to drug dealers killing each other for the privilege. A drug habit requires addicts with no visible means of support to steal from you and me. Every day. And most if not all are scared to death doing it. Legalization will change that entire dynamic.

Addicts living productive lives will reap a financial windfall. Drug prices will fall nearly 90%, as all of these drugs are very cheap to make. It would be like getting a raise. I don't know about you, but I'd rather see that money swim the mainstream economy than buy gas for BMWs driven by teenage drug barons (who, by the way, will all be out of business). Well and good, yes, but what of the addict with no visible means of support?

Those addicts remain a risk. For even with the drastic reduction in habit costs, criminal activity is the only way they can be met. But, remember, most are scared to death. And given the choice between free drugs and snatching your purse, all would take the free drugs, even if it meant living naked in an Arctic igloo. Okay, maybe not naked, but you get the picture. At least it's the picture I get when talking with hardcore addicts. And since I believe it safe to assume most of you have not had such conversations, you should probably trust me on this point. But if you don't, by all means seek one out for a chat...just keep an eye on your purse.

And for those who worry legalization will create a society awash in addiction, look to our history when drugs were abundant and legally available. Society relied upon them for a variety of ailments, over decades, and not all users became addicted. And the number that did, as a percentage of our population, remained very small – with nary a purse-snatcher among them. There were, however, judges and janitors and just about every other occupation in between.

Which is the same situation society faces now. Except now judges and janitors and all in-betweeners do business with the criminal element, not doctors and druggists. And it has quit making sense. It is time we reclaim that piece of our humanity stolen by the Bryans and Brents, time we un-burden law enforcement for the pursuit of real crime. And time to agree, however difficult it may be for some, that drug addiction is a disease.

It certainly is not difficult for me. I learned that simple truth in the Army. It was there where I first observed her-oin and its effects up close and, for a brief time, personal. My first observation revealed heroin addicts to be a pretty secretive and solitary bunch. Heroin isn't exactly a party drug, unless everyone at the party is doing heroin, which makes for a pretty boring event – conversation is difficult when most everyone is nodding out. And they're about as dangerous as a puppy in a pet shop, though many are as forlorn.

At our nuclear missile site in West Germany, we had two heroin addicts functioning well enough to avoid Captain Wilson's initial clean sweep. Which was my second observation: heroin addicts can be productive and reliable. One addict was motor pool's best mechanic, able to take apart and reassemble an engine with his eyes closed, which, at times, came in handy. He was also one of the best springboard divers this side of the Olympics.

Our other addict held a high-profile position, which is why I won't reveal specifics, other than to say it was mission critical. He was bright and funny and played a pivotal role in passing our Inspector General Review. We hit it off. Many nights we would sit behind the secure doors of his command post, him doing heroin and me asking how come. His normal childhood wasn't the answer. Neither was the fact he lived life on the right side of the law. It was nothing like that.

It was more the fact he felt a nagging void, one he was never able to put his finger on, just always there. Booze didn't fill it, which would have made his life simpler, but heroin did – that very first time. His praise for heroin would have made Bayer proud, but he was not lost to the irony of doing something to feel better that, given half a chance, would kill him. With the fluctuating purity of black market heroin, accidental overdose becomes a constant hazard, a certain cruel and unusual punishment.

But with all the hashish and good German beer to go around, heroin use at our nuclear missile site was negligible. A few curious soldiers here and there, but nothing of any real consequence. And it was the same among German friends I made over the course of my travels, leading to my next observation: heroin can be a take it *and* leave it proposition. In fact, absent any nagging void, heroin has little lasting appeal. And what little appeal it may have, it certainly isn't the vomiting part – a fairly common reaction.

I sure didn't like it.

It wasn't some nagging void that led me to try heroin, but rather I simply wanted to compare it to opium. The circumstances surrounding the satisfaction of my curiosity are of little importance, except to say I better understood the secretive and solitary part. And to say I did enough heroin that any genetic predisposition to addiction would have been satisfied as well. All of which led to my final observation: heroin ain't for the healthy – or the sick. And that it is no more effective (or debilitating) than morphine, as many doctors of the early 1900s rightly stated. Heroin was unnecessary, a product of ignorance and failed medicine – a mistake we can easily correct.

Consider this: if opiate addicts could buy morphine cheap and pure and over the counter, a black market in heroin could not compete, much less thrive. Street heroin is heavily adulterated, never pure, maybe 60% if you're lucky. And even if it were pure, they'd have to damn near give it away. Any MBA case study of a business that must nearly double quality while reducing prices 90%, and then sell to fewer customers, would be a short one. And, remember, all heroin addicts prefer the path of least resistance: walking into the corner drug store is easier than ducking down an alleyway.

It's like buying Cuban cigars in Cuba. You can buy them in licensed shops or on the black market. But street stogies are often factory seconds or mislabeled counterfeits, all with no more than a dollar or so discount to those sold in the finest shops, already at prices that make you pinch yourself. All of which made black market cigars a real tough sell, much the same way legal morphine would affect black market heroin. And, yes, it is a small step – but one in the right direction. Eliminating heroin from the market place will not alter the face of opiate addiction, but will make it kinder.

Now consider this: if raw opium and laudanum were once again legal and accessible, that face of addiction could be kinder still. Opiates are like alcohol: one size doesn't fit all. Extra-strength is not always necessary, suggesting the disease has pathogens both weak and strong. For many alcoholics, beer works just fine, even with equal availability to hard liquor. And for many addicts, given again the choice, opium and laudanum would suffice, reserving morphine for the strongest of pathogens.

And if you don't want to consider either of the above, know this: Of the amount of heroin consumed in the world, the United States accounts for no more than 5%. But we pay the highest retail price, ensuring the very last kilo of heroin on the face of the earth will be sold to America. Which means, in essence, we must first reduce the world's heroin consumption 95% before the slightest claim of victory here at home has any credibility. All in a time when we can't even keep it out of our prisons.

So when our politicians tell us they've got heroin on the run, they're lying. And what's more, they know it. But they're stuck in ideological quicksand, unable to pull themselves free. They insist addicts are not sick but just weak in character, and that a trip or two to the woodshed will straighten them out. Yet they've been taking addicts to the woodshed for nearly a hundred years now, spending hundreds of billions of dollars in the process, all the while failing miserably to straighten anyone – or anything – out.

We can end all this stupidity. We can begin by taking those politicians to the only woodshed they understand, the voting booth. We can tell them we've heard enough, demanding no other voice but that of reason be heeded. We can tell them we've seen enough crime and death and disease that drug prohibition visits upon society. We can tell them we are no longer afraid. We can tell them our courage flows from truth, and they stand alone in their quicksand. And we must tell them in no uncertain terms. Soon.

Because we'll never get rid of that 95%. The key is in actually doing the opposite, giving our 5% back to the world. And we do it through a commonsense policy of selling or otherwise providing pure morphine to our heroin addicts. It is as simple as it sounds. Not that first heroin addict will continue shopping the black market, with all its vagaries, with fear being the best example, when legal access to a qualitatively and quantifiably better product exists. Such a policy may not please everyone, but only the most rabid anti-drug moralist will object to the elimination of heroin from America's streets.

But screw 'em. They're the ones who got us into this mess in the first place: Bishop Brent, William Jennings Bryan and, last but certainly not least, William Randolph Hearst. It was not the voice of God commanding their actions, but rather echoes of their internal mutterings of religious bigotry and racism, bad seeds both, bearing hybrid fruit like Henry J. Anslinger and Richard M. Nixon. And none of it tastes very good.

Screw them all.

NAKED TRUTH IX

Cocaine

The coca plant, much like the poppy, has been around for ages. It is one of nature's most durable creations, resistant to drought and disease. And in its native habitat it doesn't even require irrigation. It just grows. The earliest mention dates back 5,000 years, when South American Indians discovered simply chewing a wad of coca leaves produced mild euphoria and increased stamina, making life at higher altitudes all the better. I know this is getting redundant, but they considered coca a gift from their gods. So did the Peruvian Incas. They cultivated large coca plantations, using the harvest in all religious ceremonies and for just about everything else. Life was pretty good.

And then the Spaniards showed up. Defeating the more primitively armed Incas, the invading conquistadors took possession of all coca plantations. When Spanish priests traveling with the warriors found natives more interested in coca than Christ, the Catholic Church outlawed its use, labeling it "an evil agent of the Devil." Also redundant.

But the Church soon changed its tune when Incans, deprived of their coca, became easily fatigued and unproductive workers, especially in the gold mines. And since doing God's work didn't come cheap, the Catholics turned cultivators, supplying coca to miners during frequent breaks. The new landlords were allowed to pay their Spanish taxes in coca leaf, introducing it to Western culture. We liked it too, although it wasn't long before, as seemed to be our wont, we sought to make it better. And what we got is cocaine.

That was around 1860. Albert Niemann (1834-1861), a chemist at the University of Gottingen in Germany, isolated coca's active ingredient, naming it cocaine. He died shortly after – the record is unclear how – and it would be another twenty years before ophthalmologists discovered cocaine to be the perfect local anesthetic. It was Viennese eye surgeon Karl Koller (1857-1944) who first popularized the practice, and the medical world took notice. So did the military.

In 1883 the Bavarian Army tasked German physician Theodore Aschenbrant with finding a military advantage in cocaine. Soldiers given cocaine remained normal in every respect, but endurance and performance levels were greatly enhanced. Seemed like a winner. Results of his study were published in a German medical journal, catching the eye of an ambitious Viennese neurologist, the infamous Sigmund Freud. To say Freud liked cocaine would be a considerable understatement.

Freud became cocaine's rainmaker, being paid by rival pharmaceutical companies to extol its virtues. And extol he did. He wrote enthusiastically about cocaine, most notably *Uber Coca* (1884), where many of cocaine's medicinal benefits were correctly identified. He missed the mark badly, however, suggesting cocaine as an effective treatment for morphine and alcohol addiction, resulting in damage to his professional reputation. He suffered personally as well, something his own addiction to cocaine bears out. But Freud wasn't the only one enamored with cocaine.

Sir Arthur Conan Doyle, speaking through Sherlock Holmes in his second novel, *The Sign of Four,* praised cocaine as "so transcendentally stimulating and clarifying to the mind that its secondary action [addiction] is a matter of small moment." Maybe. And Robert Louis Stevenson is said to have written, perhaps prophetically, *The Strange Case of Dr. Jekyll and Mr. Hyde* in just days while coked-out of his skull. Writers...

And, of course, there were the businessmen. One enterprising Corsican, Angelo Mariani (1838-1914), developed a coca libation that proved to be a worldwide hit. It was in 1863 when Mariani discovered adding small amounts of cocaine to wine produced an invigorating tonic, one he labeled Vin Mariani. Kings and Queens and a pope or two sang its praises, even Thomas Edison is said to have given glowing testimonials.

Not to be outdone by European counterparts, American entrepreneurs soon developed their own cocaine-laced tonics. The most successful was Atlanta physician John Stith Pemberton. Considered brilliant – medical degree at 19, set professional standards for licensing Georgia's pharmacists, built a highly regarded laboratory for the analysis and manufacture of chemicals – Pemberton had but one obsession: create the ultimate medicinal drink. It would be his legacy. And if he made a few bucks, that was okay too.

Knowledgeable of coca's history as a stimulant, and a connoisseur of Mariani's wine, Pemberton sought to do Mariani one better. To his own wine and cocaine tonic he added the kola nut and a dash of damiana, reputed to be a potent aphrodisiac. When he believed the formula just right, "Pemberton's French Wine Coca" came to market. That was 1886. And while sold primarily as a nerve tonic, the subtle suggestion of sex was not lost on many imbibers. Sales were brisk – for about a year.

Then the temperance movement turned Atlanta dry. Pemberton's French Wine Coca was prohibited, sending its inventor back to the drawing board. Keeping the cocaine and the kola nut, Pemberton worked feverishly to find alternatives for the wine component. But when Atlanta's prohibition act was repealed just a year later, Pemberton resumed selling his wine coca, leaving long-time associate Asa Candler to finalize the project. Candler hired Frank Robinson, Pemberton's former partner, and the two perfected the formula. And they named it Coca-Cola.

Now, we'll find out who really shot Kennedy before the Coca-Cola Company admits the real Classic Coke contained cocaine, but Pemberton claimed his new soft drink still retained "the valuable tonic and nerve stimulant properties of the coca plant and cola nuts." Corner drugstores in Atlanta installed the first counters where stopping by for a nickel shot of Coke became a very popular social ritual, and not everyone was just plain thirsty. An interesting irony is Coca-Cola became *the* drink of temperance crusaders.

And by 1895 Coca-Cola was enjoyed in every corner of the United States. But the anti-drug fever of the early 1900s brought Coca-Cola under intense scrutiny. The company responded vigorously, arguing their formula utilized only a flavor extract of the coca leaf. Okay. But their formula remained secret, allowing Coca-Cola to say "trust me on this one," and government apparently did. Whatever the truth was at the time, undoubtedly no cocaine remained in Pemberton's legacy after the Harrison Narcotics Act of 1914.

Prior to that legislative lunacy, cocaine enjoyed wide use and acceptance. It was in everything from toothache drops to dandruff cures, with one very popular seller, Ryno's Hay Fever and Catarrh Remedy, being 99% pure cocaine. But not everyone taking cocaine became addicted, and most of those who did were alcoholics or morphine addicts buying into another failed promise. Cocaine did not seem the menace to society morphine was thought to be, and almost didn't make it into Harrison. Almost.

Abraham Lincoln issued the Emancipation Proclamation in 1863, freeing the slaves. We were still fighting the Civil War though, and not everyone paid attention, especially those down South. The war ended but the peace was messy, making clear the need for more than just a proclamation. So Lincoln saw to it the 13th Amendment became the law of the land, December 6, 1865. The South wasn't entirely convinced. Life continued, however, and many blacks found employment unloading ships steaming into southern ports. The money wasn't very good, but they got free cocaine.

That seems to have been the idea of Dr. Hamilton Wright, a man knowledgeable of coca's history, and one he sold to dock bosses as a means to increase productivity. It worked of course, pleasing management no end. Cocaine followed the dockworkers home, providing a recreational pastime at a time when there was little else in the way of entertainment. They were certainly not amused by the Ku Klux Klan or seeing more black men than fruit hanging from trees, twin atrocities at their peak in the 1890s.

That was the climate. For most Southern white men, still decades from embracing cocaine like a long-lost brother, demonizing cocaine to further stigmatize blacks was a natural. For added effect, they tossed in the fact a black man high on cocaine would rape every white woman in sight. And when they weren't busy raping, they were killing. "Drug crazed Negroes fire on everyone in sight in a Mississippi town," read one local headline, noting, in all capital letters, three white men were among the dead.

Cocaine use was banned, but just in the South and only if you were black. A cocaine black market developed, more inflammatory newspaper articles appeared, and the police sprang into action. Soon it was reported black men under cocaine's influence were impervious to standard police ammunition, spurring the development of deadlier bullets. Amidst all this racial hysteria, Southern states demand the government make cocaine possession a federal crime.

But a government preoccupied with Bishop Brent and his opium crusade paid scant attention to this relatively new drug, and besides, white northerners on cocaine weren't crazed or fiendish. It had to be a black thing. And since most blacks lived in the South, we adopted an "out of sight, out of mind," mentality. It was enough to deal with all those dangerous Chinese and their opium, so we took a pass. This did not make the South happy. They needed to find a way to scare us up North, and found a surprising ally.

And in what may help explain why the *New York Times* allowed Jayson Blair to lie and falsify his reporting for so long, the *Times*, on February 8, 1914, just as Harrison was being debated in Congress, ran this helpful headline: "Negro Cocaine Fiends New Southern Menace." We got scared. Cocaine was quickly added to Harrison, and, unlike with morphine, Congress ascribed no medicinal value to the coca leaf, despite reasoned argument to the contrary. It was completely outlawed.

During the fifteen years following Harrison, cocaine took a backseat to heroin. And with the introduction of legal – and cheaper – amphetamines in the 30s, use dropped precipitously and all but disappeared by the 50s. It resurfaced in the 60s and became the life of the party in the 70s, when the demographic of drug users skewed to white and middle-class. So Congress, now more scared than ever, ratified Nixon's Comprehensive Drug Abuse Prevention and Control Act, classifying cocaine a Schedule II drug.

Which is interesting, as Schedule II drugs, though tightly controlled, are considered to have medicinal value. This contradicted Harrison, correctly, but classified cocaine as less dangerous than marijuana, a Schedule I drug. Yes, our government says marijuana is more dangerous than cocaine. Now, I have more fond memories than otherwise of my extended courtship with cocaine, but I didn't snort enough to believe that. Did you? Did anyone?

Yet cocaine did have its defenders. One drug expert, Dr. Peter G. Bourne, who would later advise Jimmy Carter on health issues, wrote in 1974 that cocaine is "benign... not physically addicting, and acutely pleasurable." Well, maybe. But only in the context presented in the 1980 *Comprehensive Textbook of Psychiatry,* which stated snorting cocaine several times a week posed little danger. And when you take all the *Miami Vice* away, that was pretty much the experience of most cocaine users. We tried it, many of us liked it and, when the thrill was gone, most of us moved on.

Drug laws didn't keep us from cocaine, obviously, but neither did they play a part in our quitting. Of course there were those who chose to indulge beyond reason, often finding themselves estranged from both friends and family, seeking new relationships based solely on cocaine. But their numbers were small. That is not to dismiss cocaine as a danger, but only to say the average experience, if not entirely benign, was of small consequence. And let's not forget the many, many among us who rejected cocaine after snorting just one line – okay, maybe two – thinking the whole thing a big waste of time.

But our government thought otherwise. It is now 1980. Ronald Reagan is president. He strays from his fundamental belief that government is too large and intrusive, and gives the DEA extraordinary powers, backed by unprecedented taxpayer funding. From the White House he tells us cocaine is ruining America. Nancy Reagan tells us to "Just Say No." And though it wasn't the last laugh, we laugh anyway and keep snorting. The Medellin cocaine cartel in Columbia is having the best laugh, making billions. Time flies. And all of a sudden it's 1985.

Those five short years are a very illustrative roadmap to our current situation. To get the DEA's story, go to www.dea.gov/deamuseum/1980-1985.htm. Titled *A Tradition of Excellence,* everyone should read it. Here the DEA reveals not only their infrastructure and strategy, but actual operations – code names and all. And while it is a best-foot forward approach, abundantly clear is why the drug war has been a complete failure: bloated bureaucracy vs. highly motivated individuals. The handwriting was on the wall,

America, it just wasn't in braille. And it said we were headed to hell.

And it was crack cocaine that ushered us through the gates. Once upon a time, "rocking-up" and smoking cocaine was just something volume buyers did to test purity levels. It was simple, safe, and a reliable gauge. While I don't believe we can pin the tail on the actual donkey responsible for first marketing crack, we can explore several scenarios as to why it went retail.

The first is that crack cocaine seems to have a longer shelf life. Powder cocaine, if not properly stored, loses potency. One response by the Medellin cartel to Reagan's drug war escalation in the 80s was to ship as much cocaine as possible into the United States, playing the odds. Getting more through than anticipated, the cartel may have resorted to crack simply as a way of preserving inventory. The DEA likes that idea, but fails to understand their complicity in crack's popularity, as the cartels were responding to a threat, not a demand.

Dumb luck aside, demand quickly became an issue, as smoking crack produced an indescribable high. It doesn't pass Go or collect $200: it goes straight to your brain. And while it remains debatable smoking is more addictive than snorting, there exists little argument pleasure derived from crack cocaine drives one's desire to consume more. The effect is almost instantaneous, wildly euphoric yet short in duration – hence the craving. Now, if it were only profitable.

That crack cocaine was *more* profitable than powder added to the dumb luck and demand and created the perfect storm. The cartels, almost at every turn, succeeded in outwitting the DEA, shipping America vast amounts of cocaine, converting much of it to crack. Both plentiful and, compared to powder, cheap, crack was popular but hardly the epidemic proclaimed by the DEA. How could it be, when, at the same time, their data indicate 95% of the population seemed immunized simply by exercising common sense?

That may not be what the DEA would like you to conclude after reading their next installment of *A Tradition of Excellence,* covering the years 1985-1990. But considering the percentage of population using cocaine has varied narrowly in either direction since, there is little else to surmise. Except that the bureaucracy became even more bloated, creating Task Force this and Task Force that, spending many hundreds of millions more taxpayer dollars in the process – by any measure all a failed effort. But don't take my word for it, go to www.usdoj.gov/dea/deamuseum/dea-history-book/1985-1990.htm and read it for yourself. Then you decide if much has really changed.

And while there may be no success like failure, failure is no success at all. We have gone from spending hundreds of millions to billions, still running the fool's errand. Our inner cities are crime scenes, their perimeters cordoned-off in yellow police tape. More cocaine comes to America than ever before, fought over and died for even as you read these words. We furlough hardened criminals early to make way for non-violent drug offenders. Yet our drug czars declare we're winning.

Well, I declare we're not. And we're not just losing. We have lost. And it is more than just the game. It is our perspective. But it can be found again, like misplaced car keys, by retracing our steps, thinking – and asking questions. Did we get sold a bill of goods or the Bill of Rights? Did all those folks in America slugging down a nickel shot of

Coca-Cola really go crazy, or just back to work? Did Thomas Edison get burnt-out on cocaine, or just more bright ideas? And did all those voices lead us to salvation, or just astray?

Perspective. Cocaine should not be taken lightly, but, the reality is, it can be taken. It is a substance, when consumed in moderation, many find pleasurable. And that is the real world experience of the overwhelming majority of users. It is the responsible use theory in action. Yes, there are those who consume far past moderation. But so what. We don't jail drunks just for drinking, do we? No, we do so only when the public safety is compromised, mostly by drunk drivers. Cocaine use should be treated no differently.

And while I have no sympathy for those caught driving under any influence, someone behind several lines of coke poses far less danger than anyone after a six-pack of beer. Cocaine, much like Ritalin, tends to focus the user, whereas alcohol, as many of us well know, blurs. That said, I believe our criminal justice system is guilty of lax enforcement of current DUI laws, allowing many violators to plead to a lesser charge. Put every offender in jail for a minimum of three days, longer when there is property damage or personal injury. Now that's a zero-tolerance policy I could get behind.

The long and the short of my courtship with cocaine is that I did it, liked it a lot, then quit. Never free-based, never smoked crack, though I had sufficient opportunity. Over a period of about eighteen months I snorted close to ten ounces of cocaine, or an average of three grams a week. I held a responsible position in a rapidly growing company that was drug friendly but all business. I did cocaine with white-collars and blue-collars alike. It was all very social, pleasant. Then I simply stopped, but it sure was fun while it lasted.

That was twenty years ago. And maybe it did take a few years off my life. Maybe not. Either way, I posed absolutely no danger to society. It was society that presented the greatest danger, in the form of misguided drug policy. Being convicted for possession of cocaine, even personal use amounts, was a felony and the random ruin of too many otherwise ordinary lives. And nothing has changed, twenty years later.

And nothing will change in the next twenty years unless society demands the order our laws are meant to provide. America's drug policies have produced nothing but chaos, screwing the pooch for ninety years. Are we tired yet? I know the pooch is. So let's stop. Repeal Harrison and the Comprehensive Drug Abuse Prevention and Control Act. Abolish the Drug Enforcement Administration. Just wipe the slate clean. Begin again by allowing, again, the legal sale of cocaine, understanding it to be an adult pleasure while educating our children to its peril. Cash-out the cartels, end the crime. It is time.

Let Pemberton have his legacy.

NAKED TRUTH X

Doing the math

Trying to calculate the amount of money America has expensed fighting drugs gave me headaches. If every piece of existing financial data were to be stacked tight inside containers of 18-wheelers, we'd have ourselves a country-mile convoy. But even with the brightest green-eyeshade guys doing the diligence, that old adage "figures lie and liars figure" would make finding a hard number difficult. That we have so far spent many tens of billions seems a safe bet, but what we *have* spent is not the point. What we *will* spend is the more sobering number, and should be our focus.

Let's begin with the year 2003. It took an aspirin or two, but I figured fifty billion to be a fair estimate, though some claim it much higher. Yet I doubt anyone knowledgeable in this area would claim it less, or deny drug budgets increase every year. But to illustrate my point, I've chosen a more conservative number for 2003: forty billion. To that amount I have added a modest 8% yearly increase, and calculated

America's cost over the next ninety years, borne partly by us baby boomers but laid heavily upon our children and theirs.

To keep things simple, we'll examine ten years at a time. In the year 2013, with many boomers still footing the bill, our drug budget will be eighty billion dollars, doubling. More telling is that by the end of 2013, our aggregate spending for the decade will total five hundred thirty-nine billion, six hundred million dollars. That's nearly enough to fund the entire Medicare prescription drug plan. Sorry, mom. And we'll have more crime, though the percentage of addicts will remain fairly static, same for recreational users.

The national budget for 2014 will be eighty-six billion, four hundred million dollars. And over the next decade, when most boomers quit paying taxes and our children begin the heavy lifting, drug war spending will total one trillion, one hundred sixty-six billion dollars. Merry Christmas, kids – now pay up. And don't forget to write, especially all those Social Security checks. By the end of that decade, just twenty years from now, our aggregate total will be one trillion, seven hundred and five billion dollars. And we'll have more crime, though the percentage of addicts will remain fairly static, same for recreational users.

Beginning the third decade, in 2024, our drug budget will be one hundred eighty-six billion, four hundred million dollars. And if you think we treat our elders shabbily now, just wait. It isn't very difficult to imagine our kids tapping their watches, wondering just how much longer we'll live. In this decade we will spend a total of two trillion, seven hundred and one billion dollars. By the end of that decade, just thirty years from now, our aggregate total will be four trillion, four hundred and six billion dollars. And we'll have more crime, though the percentage of addicts will remain fairly static, same for recreational users.

Anyone see a pattern developing here? Anyone believe we could better spend those four trillion tax dollars, and the thirty-six trillion more over the full ninety-year span? Because we're going to spend that forty trillion, you know, one way or the other. And the other way makes more sense.

Think Homeland Security. Social Security. Education. Medicare and Medicaid. Alzheimer's. HIV/AIDS. Stem cells and terrorist cells. Better military pay, and payloads. Then think about Nero, fiddling as the fires raged through Rome.

Ah, but what the hell. It's only money.

NAKED TRUTH XI

Who *are* these guys?

Ever wonder just where our government gets all the data influencing existing drug policy? Okay, so you don't. But do any of those polling calls you get at dinner ask your opinions on drug policy? Me either. But they have to be talking to someone, right? As wrongheaded as our drug policy is, it doesn't happen in a vacuum. It begins at the National Drug Intelligence Center, an independent component inside our Department of Justice. Created during the Clinton administration, the NDIC issues an annual *National Drug Threat Assessment,* combining "foreign and domestic counter-drug intelligence and information on domestic drug trends in a single report." Just the facts, ma'am...

The NDIC director is one Michael T. Horn, appointed in 1999 by then Attorney General Janet Reno. A formidable looking fellow, Horn first entered government service in 1968, working for the Bureau of Narcotics and Dangerous Drugs. When the BNDD morphed into the DEA, he went along, rising through the ranks to become in 1977 Special Agent in Charge for the newly opened Atlantic City Resident office. Two years later came his promotion to run the DEA joint Federal-local narcotic task force in Philadelphia. Next was ten years as DEA Country Attaché in various foreign lands, earning more stripes.

In 1991 Mr. Horn was tapped by the DEA to head its Technical Operations Section. Five years later the DEA anointed him Chief of Special Operations Division, giving him the reins to a pretty big wagon. The Special Operations Division bossed the FBI and the US Customs Service in a joint effort to combine everybody's everything, creating this streamlined machine to fight the drug war. I believe it safe to assume he performed well, or well enough that within a year's time the DEA offered Horn another plum.

It was in November of 1996 when the DEA awarded Horn top spot at the Office of International Operations, running their show in 70 cities inside 52 countries, seemingly the crowning achievement for a dedicated drug warrior. But the growing influence NDIC held in shaping government views drew his attention, as he saw it the pinnacle of the drug pyramid. Achieving the position in 1999, he has held it ever since. And no doubt wants to retire there. On many levels it would be a fitting legacy. Michael T. Horn is an honorable man, no buts about it.

We just disagree, that's all. And the reason why couldn't be more fundamental: though we both became interested in drugs at roughly the same time, we took diametrically opposite positions. He became the headhunter, I the hunted head. But if we were to meet today, both being at the top of our game, I can't help imagine it would be like in the movies, when two old spies in a bar take a time-out to toast the absurdity of it all. Only in the movies, they say. Instead, I'll settle for the offer Mr. Horn extends welcoming comment on his latest *National Drug Threat Assessment*, published January 2003.

I'll start with the Executive Summary. This document is usually the first few pages of any extensive report, affording our busy politicians an overview, leaving the nuts and bolts to staff – a notable distinction to make in our capitol where extensive reports are a dime a dozen. So it's reasonable to believe many politicians read only the Summary, if that. Mr. Horn estimates the number of drug-dependent Americans to be 3.2 million, or about 1.3% of our population. He states that in 2000 Americans spent nearly 64 billion dollars buying drugs, with the total cost to society being in excess of 160 billion dollars – making my forty billion estimate for 2003 seem like chump change.

And that's just in the first paragraph. In essence, we expensed over 160 billion dollars chasing less than 2% of our population spending 64 billion dollars getting high – or what our Declaration of Independence guarantees as the pursuit of happiness. That happiness is not always attained needs little discussion, as our Declaration guarantees only the *pursuit*. But it is a guarantee nonetheless. Even ignoring that little quibble, any endeavor spending 160 billion dollars in a losing proposition is just that – a losing proposition. Which gives rise to the conclusion many of our politicians just don't care, or can't read the tea leaves.

The 2003 Executive Summary ranks drugs according to their perceived danger, citing information obtained in the NDIC 2002 National Drug Threat Survey. While Mr. Horn states public health agency data are considered, Appendix A, describing NDTS methodology, mentions only the 3,002 law enforcement agency respondents. The aspect of one choir and one choirmaster aside, cocaine ranks highest as the "principal drug threat to the United States." So let's hear what Mr. Horn has to say about cocaine.

Right off the bat, he tells us powder and crack cocaine are readily available just about everywhere. And production is up, he adds, but not federal investigations, arrests or seizures. What Horn infers but dares not state is the failure of our cocaine interdiction programs. Just as telling is his confirming the numbers using powder and crack cocaine remain stable, even considering the possibility of a slight uptick among adults. It would appear increased supply and availability did not generate more users, but that existing users could be consuming more, as lower prices walk hand-in-hand with a glut in supply.

Methamphetamines rank next, also considered a "principal drug threat to the United States," except this one is mostly homegrown. Domestic production, with some inflow from Mexico, adequately supplies our demand, considered by Mr. Horn as widespread across the U.S. But it's like water on a flat rock, spread out with no depth. If it were not, the cocaine cartels would own the business, and they're nowhere to be found, at least according to Mr. Horn's Summary. I suggest this scenario reflects the miniscule number of our methamphetamine addicts, leaving a very small number of occasional users to consume what little supply remains. Mr. Horn?

Marijuana ranks third in the danger zone, labeled "a leading drug threat to the country," and the most popular guilty pleasure in the United States. Now there's a surprise. I sure hope Mr. Horn didn't spend too much money figuring that one out. Same goes for his data nugget suggesting marijuana is big business here and abroad. In fact, Mr. Horn, why are we spending *any* money on marijuana? Marijuana is not a problem. But, for the sake of argument, to agree it is a problem, surely it must be our very least. And not at all worthy of being prioritized higher than heroin, Mr. Horn.

Pinch yourself. A drug with an addict population of barely half a million that kills the highest percentage of users, more from dirty-needle AIDS than overdose, should not just be considered "a significant drug threat to the United States." That is an insult to the dead and dying, and serves only to underscore the moral judgment passed on their disposability. Perhaps your comfort comes from NDTS data suggesting overall heroin demand to be stable while actually declining in some areas, even as supply increases. At best, Mr. Horn, that is cold comfort.

MDMA, or ecstasy, ranks next. Mr. Horn, as he does with heroin, considers MDMA "a significant threat to the United States." But in all the years MDMA was legal, the only threat was having your credit card turned down by the bars selling it alongside gin and tonics. The real threat came in 1984 when MDMA was banned, allowing unprincipled manufacturers to ignore purity standards. Adulterants, primarily dextromethorphan, are what send kids to the emergency room, Mr. Horn. And with both demand and supply up, keep a sharper eye on the rearview mirror for all those flashing red lights.

At this point in his Summary, Mr. Horn bands together club drugs such as ketamine (a veterinary anesthetic), Rohypnol (a benzodiazepine), and GHB, citing their use poses a "relatively low threat in comparison" to all other drugs, including marijuana. But GHB is the date-rape drug, and every woman ever assaulted under its influence would beg to differ with Mr. Horn's assessment it poses less a threat than marijuana. What do you believe? Also included here are hallucinogens, whose use Mr. Horn concedes is quite limited. But that has always been the case, sir, and not news.

Listing pharmaceuticals last and, therefore, the least dangerous drugs in his Summary, Mr. Horn describes them "a growing drug threat to the country." Beginning with semi-synthetic morphine drugs such as hydrocodone and oxycodone, Mr. Horn takes us into Rush Limbaugh territory. But Rush was eating upwards of thirty pills a day and the only threat he presented was to Democrats. In a country more stressed by the minute, Mr. Horn then states the obvious: Xanax is the new Valium. And his assessment stimulant use is on the rise just may be the run-off from Ritalin, a drug prescribed to, and shared among, millions of our youth. Maybe the NDIC has ADD...

Anyway, Mr. Horn concludes his Executive Summary with an admission much of that 64 billion dollars spent buying drugs made a clean getaway, in a segment titled Money Laundering. All those billions are in small denominations, making bulk shipments of currency out of our country more difficult than shipping all the drugs in. But Mr. Horn believes some of the money stays here, either anonymously commingled with funds generated at legitimate businesses or blatantly blown in Vegas – or spent by 16 year-old drug dealers buying BMWs. Recommend an end to drug prohibition, Mr. Horn, and save the other 160 billion.

You may not wish to read the entire NDIC report – it was 166 pages from my printer – but do read the Summary: www.usdoj.gov/ndic/pubs3/3300/execsum.html. Not that it will make you smarter than our politicians; that's generally the case now, but you will possess the same drug intelligence they do. There is little doubt in my mind you will see what I see, or no longer need wonder who crafts the message carried by those currently running the fool's errand.

Because these are the guys.

NAKED TRUTH XII

Propaganda and Prohibition

Fighting drugs has become as much an addiction for government as heroin is to the habitual user, if not more so. And it is that addiction which must be broken first, cold turkey style. Getting government out of the drug business, and returning it to the free market system where it belongs, and began, is the only responsible course of action. But as a first order of business, we must demand an end to one of the more insidious aspects of our drug policy, the psychological warfare of propaganda. We simply must quit telling lies.

Drug propaganda has become slicker and subtler since *Reefer Madness* days, but the lies remain the same: just one puff, just one pill, just one line, just one time and your life hangs in the balance. Propagandists pry open our purse strings by tugging at our heartstrings, often shamelessly, as exemplified by a recent TV ad citing MDMA as the sole cause of a teenage girl's tragic death. She was portrayed as the quintessential girl next door, and I have no doubts she was exactly that. But I have serious doubts she consumed unadulterated MDMA, or in the massive dose necessary to cause death.

More likely is that DXM, known as the most common and most dangerous adulterant in street ecstasy, played the causative role. But that doesn't make good TV. And this was good TV. It was impossible to watch without experiencing great sadness for the family, and hearts all over our nation went out to them. My heart was no different. But my head knew it was propaganda. And that's what made me angry. Angry at a government that exploits the tragic results of their failed drug policies, pointing the finger everywhere but where it belongs, serving no higher purpose than fear-mongered fundraising.

Because our government knows unless they keep us sufficiently frightened, we will no longer fund their drug war follies. So their propaganda machine continues to roll, filling their coffers and our cemeteries. How much longer this goes on is entirely up to you and every other American, but we'd better get our big butts moving. Rumor has it frustrated drug warriors are determined to end the war once and for all, calling for measures making today's methods seem like a day at the beach. And the only thing pretty about it will be the propaganda, very slick and subtle and delivered in 30-second sound bites.

Propaganda is all about the message, and our government's message is all about how drugs are ruining America, with nothing short of our future depending on the creation of a drug-free society. Pot won't kill you, they admit, almost reluctantly, but leave no doubt it will kill your ambition and any chance of real success. All the other illegal drugs, well, that's a different story. It's a short one, and you die in the end. So you better Just Say No, O.K.? Being force-fed this steady diet for so long has inoculated us from the truth, immobilizing us, demoralizing us and, most sad of all, dehumanizing us. Propaganda: it's what's for breakfast, lunch *and* dinner.

And it is not just government propagandists wielding the spoon. Our daily newspapers are their primary co-conspirators, with few qualifying as unindictable. Their complicity in supporting government propaganda is a disgrace, blatantly hypocritical and a mockery of journalistic integrity. Even my favorite read, the *Wall Street Journal*, stands guilty. Their editorial, "An Idea Has Consequences," published May 17, 2004, is an example riddled with hypocrisy, and perhaps a bit of quid pro quo, as drugs were not mentioned at all. It was all about *Brown v. Board of Education*, the 1954 Supreme Court decision ending the educational doctrine of "separate but equal," leading to school desegregation.

The *Journal's* editors take us back fifty years, back to *Brown*, when their favorite young economist warned against assigning government, and not parents, the role in deciding where our children attend school. Instead, this young economist, now the *Journal's* favorite old economist, and mine, Milton Friedman, made the case for school vouchers, something he thoroughly articulated the following year in "The Role of Government in Education," suggesting it be a limited one. Anything more would create bureaucratic boondoggles and de facto segregation – consequences of an idea, as it were.

Consequences the *Journal* makes plain we now suffer, making even plainer the fault lies with government policies putting school choice in the hands of union and legislative bureaucrats covered with the most dirt. Listen to Milton, they say. And they seem quite pleased we are beginning to, citing the success of programs in cities like Milwaukee and Cleveland, with many more on the way. "Milton Friedman's vouchers will make *Brown's* vision real," they proclaim in bold letters. Whether they are right or wrong is not the point, at least of this exercise.

The point is this: they drank the kool-aid. And that very theory put forth in "The Role of Government in Education," which the *Journal* describes as "the intellectual equivalent of the shot heard round the world" and "the cornerstone for a fundamental civil right," is exactly the same theory Mr. Friedman repeated in 1991 in "The Drug War as a Socialist Enterprise," making the case why the drug war is a failure. So I ask the *Wall Street Journal* editors this simple question: Are you befuddled? Because I've done a lot of drugs, but only had to read both pieces once to catch Friedman's drift, and just twice to really get it. Maybe you had trouble with Adam Smith and all his "invisible hand" stuff.

Maybe not. Maybe you're just clear-minded hypocrites, engaging in a bit of cultural war quid pro quo, winking at the government's drug policy for their nod toward privatizing education. Because your position on drugs is wholly indefensible and totally inconsistent with that of Milton Friedman's, exposing an ideological rigidity no different than that of those you deride for defending the educational status quo. I'd suggest you get Milton Friedman in a room together with President Bush and drug czar John Walters and take notes, then write an editorial on the proceedings. But remember, to paraphrase George Bush, you're either with Milton Friedman or against Milton Friedman.

I single out the *Wall Street Journal* not because they are conservative and represent the right, but because such hypocrisy is beneath them. Their reporting and intellectual insight is second to none, and in the room of reason their voice is often the brightest and clearest. But when they fling themselves into the drug mosh pit of the liberal left, and then surf the wave as confidently as Teddy Kennedy, I have to wonder if someone didn't slip them a mickey. Actually, I hope that is the case. It will convince them to quit going to that kind of shindig and stick to their kool-aid.

The *Wall Street Journal* is the only newspaper in America with the journalistic pipes, not to mention the *cajones*, big enough to blow the whistle. Because the liberal press, that stalwart defender of the disenfranchised, can't do it without first having OSHA insure the whistle conforms to safety norms, and even then they won't pucker-up. No, it's up to the *Journal*. A little *mea culpa* may be in order, but it will only make them stronger. And if the deep inner reward from helping mankind end ninety years of war doesn't fulfill them completely, I have to believe the absolute joy in watching liberals chase behind their bus, flailing and shouting to wait, will. Be noble and let them on, but make them pay for gas.

And since all will undoubtedly want to sit up front, fill the empty seats with guys like Pat Robertson and Jerry Falwell and that gnomish Gary Bauer. They will be uncomfortable at first, sitting at the back of the bus and all, but they'll get over it. Because no ride can be complete without including those religious leaders and moralists sharing the same DNA as their progenitors, Bishop Brent and William Jennings Bryan. No more sweeping their dirt under the rug, no more ignoring the role religious bigotry plays.

Their righteous claim of channeling Jesus is nothing more than a cowardly abdication of all personal responsibility for their words and any deed. Jesus tells them drugs are the devil incarnate, and if we don't quit taking them there will be more than hell to pay – something like 2-10 in the federal pen. Which is pretty hard to square with their "love the sinner but hate the sin" sermon. And even harder when their children escape damnation and prison denim when caught with a pot pipe or a pocket full of pills. But their sons and daughters are different from yours and mine. Jesus tells them so.

Yet one must not forget it was religious leaders hearing voices that first led America into drug prohibition, back in the early 1900s. It was the success of Bishop Brent and his crusade against opium that emboldened William Jennings Bryan and his acolytes to champion society's arm wrestle with alcohol, an ugly struggle lasting thirteen years. And though our current struggle with drugs has lasted over eight decades longer, there are many parallels to be drawn. The obvious are crime and corruption and civil disregard for the law. Less obvious, but more telling, is that the darkest hours of Prohibition were those just before the dawn of repeal.

Crime and corruption and the costs fighting both were all at their peak. So was the debate. With one side calling for intensified enforcement, the other for outright repeal, President Hoover assigned a blue-ribbon panel the task of evaluating the situation and reporting back. The Wickersham Commission it was called, and they delivered their report in 1931, concluding "there is as yet no adequate observance or enforcement" of Prohibition. But they just thought it was because we weren't trying hard enough. They argued appropriations be substantially increased to further the good works over at the Bureau of Prohibition, so as to give law enforcement the "greatest practical efficiency."

Finally, we were going to get tough, real tough. And we did, leaving prohibitionists ecstatic. I'm not sure what kind of party they threw, but not long after the last one to leave hit the lights did another light come on and Prohibition ended. That was over 70 years ago. And now anyone proposing a return might just as well wear one of those little aluminum foil hats, for all the attention we'll pay them. It seems so silly now, but it was so deadly serious then, so dark. It is pitch-black in America again, suggesting we are in the throes of final resolution where repeal breathes the most air and prohibition takes a last breath.

Breathe deeply America. Take all the air. If we don't and allow prohibition to survive, enforcement measures will be so extreme that ...well, I really don't know how bad things will get. Because already our government can demand we defecate in a plastic bag and urinate in a paper cup in their search for drug users. But such practices, as draconian and degrading as they are, catch less than 1% of the tens of millions of Americans who take drugs. In the all-out assault now being planned, prohibitionists want the other 99%. Badly. And there is absolutely no limit to the amount of our freedom they will sacrifice to win. It is time to breathe deeply. It is time to call prohibition's bluff.

"Drugs make you criminal." Many prohibitionists will tell you that. You could be the kind of guy who wears nice sweaters and kids love, but snort a little coke and you'll lock them in the basement, hold them for ransom. Probably kill them. Really, that's what they believe. To them, addiction is not the issue. It's that first time, that first line, that keeps them up at night. They will tell you that first line causes sudden biochemical changes in the brain, manifesting as spontaneous criminal behavior. But the only criminal behavior I exhibited after snorting my first line of cocaine, though I must admit it happened rather spontaneously, was snorting my second line. Maybe they were talking about disco...

A further dispelling of the "drugs make you criminal" myth can be found in *Cocaine: A Drug and Its Social Evolution* (New York: Basic Books, 1985), authored by Lester Grinspoon and James B. Bakalar. Acknowledging cocaine, like all stimulants, can make a person jittery, they believe personality and circumstance make all the difference, concluding much aggressive behavior is predisposed and rarely predicated by drugs. Former New York City Police Deputy Chief Raymond Kelly seems to agree. He states nearly all drug violence stems from black market disputes, and not when "somebody is deranged because they're on a drug." Drugs do not make users criminal. Prohibition does.

"Only criminals do drugs." Other prohibitionists, believing themselves more astute than their "drugs make you criminal" brethren, argue cheap and legal drugs will not reduce crime, warning users will still commit crimes simply because they are criminals at heart. They contend that making drugs legal and cheap will make guns and bullets more affordable, making for more, not less, crime. That's right, they believe keeping drugs illegal lessens the frequency of crime. Are they crazy or what. I say we hunt them down but don't kill them. Just make them wear aluminum foil hats.

And then make them walk around a few days in our inner cities. Visit. Tell everyone they meet how worse life would be if not for the high price of drugs. Tell them how lucky they are. Tell them whoever keeps stealing the TV to buy $100 worth of illegal drugs will be even more determined and dangerous when legal drugs cost $10. Tell them how prohibition is a good thing. Then tell them how it's all your idea. Don't be modest and resist the temptation to take a bow. But when you look up and see murder in their eyes, be glad we made you wear that hat. Because everybody knows it's bad luck to kill a crazy person.

"God has nothing to do with it." Some prohibitionists take great pains to leave God out of the equation, simply citing the lethality of drugs as the sole reason to ban them. Were that really true, they would be absolutely anal over alcohol and tobacco, legal drugs that kill over 500,000 of us every year, or 480,000 more than all illegal drugs combined. So, lethality seems to be a red herring, an issue easily dismissed without the need for further debate. Unless, of course, they believe dying from alcoholism or lung cancer is somehow more dignified, more legally appealing, than dying from heroin addiction. Then they should keep right on talking, taking whatever pains necessary to explain how their playing God is a different equation.

Which must hurt, given all their stuttering and stammering preceding any explanation. So, for the moment, let's cede them their secular blanket, give them that comfort and cover. Because with God out of the equation, they can focus and explain why they like the deadliest drugs best. Explain their preference for alcohol and tobacco, two drugs that kill more of us every year than the total number of heroin addicts alive. Their discomfort is less on this issue, saying it really isn't their call. They defer to the wisdom of Congress, a body with more than a few Members who believe God has *everything* to do with it, making their secular claim more than a bit disingenuous. It makes it a lie.

"Legalization will addict the nation." This is the grand-daddy bluff of all prohibitionists. They say keeping drugs illegal is our only hope, our only prayer, to keep the lid on. Like the only thing stopping over 98% of us from running out and shooting heroin or smoking cocaine is respect for the law. Such a premise is not only an affront to our collective common sense, it represents a direct threat to our common good. It may have been a surprise to you Sears sold a little heroin next to their hammers, and that the addiction rate then was no greater than today, and that drug crime was non-existent, but it is no surprise to them. To knowingly create a false climate of fear is tantamount to treason. But to perpetuate it by war *is* treason.

Je t'accuse...

NAKED TRUTH XIII

Legalization

Making us safe from the harm of drugs systematically made us less safe, to the point today where we are the least safe. And tomorrow will only be worse. Our drug policy has fostered a lack of respect for others and their property, both tenets of normative behavior absolutely essential for public safety. Our prisons are not only overcrowded with drug offenders, they are overrun with drugs as well. Tell me it's not all insane. Then tell me I'm insane to believe repealing drug prohibition will be the most significant law and order legislation of the 21st century.

The United States led the world into drug prohibition, and it is the United States that can lead us all out. Some believe legalization will turn America into the world's magnet for drug users. And it just might. But not for long. Removing the United States from the black market in drugs will shrink the traffickers' pie to crumbs, forcing them to greatly intensify efforts elsewhere. Bet on it getting ugly

very quickly. And that most countries will follow our enlightened lead, some even questioning why it took so long.

It's the old "think globally, act locally" scenario. So let's
think globally for a minute. All the world's cocaine comes
from South America, where guerilla armies and cartels control production and distribution. America consumes 85% of
their product, creating a yearly cash flow of over a hundred
billion dollars, financing an awful lot of mortars and man-
sions. When U.S. legalization pinches that nerve, watch
how fast they get spastic. And when they're still twitching,
exposed and weak, watch how fast the rest of the world joins
the kill. It will be instinctive.

Heroin is different, in that America consumes just 5%
of global production. Even though we pay heroin's highest price, eliminating our black market will not change the
global dynamics of heroin. The renegade military generals,
drug lords and warlords running the trade will remain in
business and unwilling to go away quietly. They can only
be defeated when made irrelevant, something easily accomplished through the global legalization of morphine. And if
you think that sounds crazy, then go find me the addict who
will risk buying impure heroin at high prices from criminals
when given the option of pure morphine on the cheap from
corner drugstores. Really, go look. But pack a lunch.

The global trafficking in cocaine and heroin is unques-
tionably the most violent sector of the drug black market,
due to the sheer enormity of profits. Territory is hard won
and defended to the death. Killing is a job description, and
assassination an occupational hazard. So it is both foolish and naïve to believe enacting the death penalty against
drug dealers, an option more frequently discussed these
days, will act as a deterrent. It will only ratchet up their vi-

olence, eliminating what little else they have to lose. Global legalization is the only way to end the carnage.

Global legalization is not the magic bullet, but it is a magic wand. Wave it over the world and watch whole societies stabilize. The quiet desperation of drug addiction will remain, but black market violence will disappear. So will all the official corruption, much to the chagrin of all corrupt officials. Global law enforcement will better protect and serve, chasing the real bad guys and catching more of them. And the world will be a healthier place: injecting drugs with clean needles will slow our spread of HIV/AIDS faster than any cocktail on the pharmaceutical drawing board. What's not to like?

The messenger, perhaps. There will be those who dismiss my global perspective as the ranting of a man deranged by thirty-plus years of taking drugs. Fair enough. But what about men like George Shultz, secretary of state for Ronald Reagan, or Walter Cronkite, long considered "America's most trusted man," or good old Milton Friedman, recipient of the 1976 Nobel Prize for Economics? Are they deranged? Because they're all singing pretty much the same tune: in a public letter to U.N. Secretary-General Kofi Annan, those three distinguished men, along with 500 other world luminaries, called for a more sane and humane approach to the global drug crisis.

The letter was written June 1, 1998, a week before the United Nations General Assembly Special Session on Drugs convened in New York, and sought Kofi Annan's leadership in stimulating a "frank and honest" assessment of global drug control efforts. In it, the signatories add just one caveat: in order to be frank and honest, the United Nations must be willing to address tough questions as to the success or failure of its past efforts. Efforts the letter sum up in a dramatic one-sentence paragraph: "We believe that the global war on drugs is now causing more harm than drug abuse itself."

They support this position by pointing out that every decade the United Nations adopts new global drug policies focused mainly on criminalization and punishment, restricting individual countries from devising effective solutions to local problems. This forces world governments every year to enact more punitive and more costly drug control measures, leading politicians every day to endorse even deadlier drug war strategies. And their evidence is pretty convincing, some of which the United Nations supplied.

U.N. agencies estimate the annual revenue generated by the illegal drug industry at nearly four hundred billion dollars, or the equivalent of roughly 8% of total international trade. As a result, the letter states, this drug industry has "empowered organized crime, corrupted governments at all levels, eroded international security, stimulated violence, and distorted both economic markets and moral values." And they make clear this is the consequence of decades of failed drug war policies, not drug use per se.

In addition, they fault drug war politics for impeding world health initiatives, for defoliating the environment and violating human rights, all in the delusional attempt to create drug-free societies. They warn Secretary-General Annan of more drugs, more drug crime, more disease and suffering should the world stay the course. They ask he stand tall against those who will accuse him of " surrendering," labeling true surrender as when fear and rigidity combine to kill all debate, discredit all critics and dismiss any alternative offered.

It would seem to even the casual reader of the letter that global drug prohibition has been a huge and utter failure, a social experiment long passed its expiration date. And that only a global policy of legalization will lead us away from our madness. Okay, they don't actually use the word "legalization," a word George Shultz once wryly noted as one that turns drug warriors deaf and dumber. But they do call for a global drug policy to "reduce the harms associated with drugs," a new policy in which "fear, prejudice and punitive prohibitions yield to common sense, science, public health and human rights." Smells like legalization to me. Take a whiff yourself: www.lindesmith.org/news/un.html

The only problem I have with the letter is that it was sent to Kofi Annan. This was a man up to his whiskers in weasels, doing lunch with Saddam Hussein and the bidding for Yasir Arafat, all the while granting repressive states like Syria a seat on the U.N. Human Rights Commission. I mean, come on. This is not exactly the guy you want downfield when you throw humanity's Hail Mary pass. And in the ensuing six years since George Shultz et al. penned their plea, Kofi Annan has not distinguished himself or the United Nations in any substantive way, least of all in dealing with the global drug crisis. Read the letter again, Mr. Annan. Then stand tall or go back to Ghana.

As for the rest of us, we need to start asking what gives. Why are such bright and somber individuals, many world-renowned, routinely ignored? There has to be a reason. Perhaps the answer is rooted in this simple question: Who benefits from the drug war? Whenever I ask this question, the near-unanimous response is "drug dealers." That is technically correct but not completely correct. As the global infrastructure to fight drugs continues to grow exponentially, government bureaucrats enlarge their fiefdoms and loathe seeing them shrink. It is arguable they care more for their private turf than the public square. So don't expect them to go away any more quietly than their strange bedfellows, the traffickers.

Drug dealers and drug warriors. They are the real winners. And one of the few things setting them apart is that drug dealers keep all the money we give them. Drug warriors do not. Either way, it's all our money. And we keep giving it to them, prima facie evidence proving us the real losers. But it's more than just the money. It is the personal loss. We now have over two million prisoners in our penal system, second only to Russia, with 60% being non-violent drug offenders, many as average as any Joe. Talk to their families. Ask them if they consider their spouse or child criminal. Ask them if our drug laws make any sense. They won't be hard to find. They're already on the bus.

And ours is not the Who's *Magic Bus,* a song of yearning for something good, with the words "I want it, I want it" repeated over and over in increasing urgency only to be told "you can't have it," stretching the word can't as if to rub it in. No, our bus is different. But we too yearn for something good. We yearn for an end to warring against ourselves and beginning a new day a different way. We've long felt it in our hearts but now it's in our bones. We must tell our politicians so, repeatedly and urgently and not let them tell us we can't have it. Not anymore. Tell them they're either on the bus or off the bus.

Our passenger list cannot be considered complete without the inclusion of another group, one I call "the friendlies." The friendlies are all those on the forefront of medical marijuana, an issue of great validity. But they are wasting all their time and money on tests and studies to bring reason to the unreasonable when they should be shaking them by the shoulders and screaming *"Are you nuts?"* Current drug czar John Walters was on TV the other day doing a dead-on impersonation of Henry Anslinger, our first drug czar, stating unequivocally that marijuana is a menace to society. This man is running our drug war. This man is nuts.

And so are the friendlies. Many smoke marijuana themselves, and all are not AIDS or glaucoma sufferers. As such, it's been said medical marijuana advocates are selfishly exploiting the hopes of the sick and dying, attempting to legalize marijuana through a back door. While this accusation is beneath contempt, it is to be expected in a debate long passed all reason and civility. But all you friendlies need to come out of the closet on recreational marijuana and support the many millions of us supporting you. Stand all the way up. In fact, take on the whole fight and demand an end to all drug prohibition. Help make us all well. To do any less would be, well, you know...nuts.

Let's play a game. Let's say the *Wall Street Journal* did blow the whistle and start the bus rolling. And, despite fretting the bus had no seat belts, the liberals ended up happy buying all the gas. Even say the religious right got comfortable taking a back seat for a change. We'll say the bureaucrats and drug warriors all landed on their feet, once they came to, and that the friendlies became even more so. Let's say all of that. Let's say America breathes deeply and drug prohibition is repealed. The game starts now. But what will legalization look like, how will it all work? And will we screw it all up? How it looks and works will determine that. So let's keep playing.

First, let's be reminded we are not playing blind. The 19th century ushered in the great promise of prosperity and, by and large, we realized it. Opium, laudanum, morphine, heroin and cocaine were legally available and cheap. Smoking opium and sipping laudanum went somewhat public, though intravenous drug use remained a private matter. Cocaine wines were socially popular, and virtually everyone enjoyed the true classic Coke. Yet with all that freedom of choice the addiction rate was miniscule, no greater than today. The social stigma attached to drug addiction was less than what we ascribed to alcoholism, rightly considered the greater problem. And what we had then is what we now seek, no drug crime. That's what we're playing for.

So let's consider that our basic playbook. We'll need to make a few changes though. Opium, morphine and cocaine will be legally available to adults, all without the need for a prescription, but it will be a pharmacist and not a mailman handling the transaction. No more mail order. Which makes drugstore chains the obvious choice, as they are within a few miles of just about everyone. But so are retailers like Wal-Mart, and they have pharmacies. So do many grocery stores. My bet is retailers, especially Wal-Mart, opt out, viewing the products as inappropriate as some music and magazines already barred from their shelves. And that grocery stores may have no choice but to opt out: with a comparatively small customer base, there just won't be all that much business to go around.

And what about the local watering holes? Should they be able to serve a cocaine and wine cocktail, ala Vin Mariani? Sure, why not. Because we sure can't stop drinking and driving. And in such an imperfect world, I'd rather follow someone with a little cocaine in their tank. So should you.

What about a non-alcoholic cola with a pinch of cocaine? Of course, but coffee futures may take a hit. And a little opium in your merlot? Again, why not. But liquor stores will do the lion's share of that business, not bars. The effect of laudanum is more conducive to listening to Rachmaninoff or watching *Blazing Saddles,* activities that keep you on the couch and not behind the wheel. And when you wake up, it won't be in the hospital.

Nor will it be Xanadu. All of a sudden we will have a portion of our addict population in flux, no longer forced to pay high prices for drugs but still without the means to afford cheap ones. And no one is going to offer them jobs. But in all fairness to corporate America, these addicts won't want one. All they want is to do drugs and be left alone. We should let them. A national system of drug asylums, where addicts can live out their lives in relative peace, where society is held harmless, is the humane way to accomplish this feat. And it will be an absolute bargain, as the infrastructure is mostly in place.

Since 1988, the Defense Department and Congress have engaged in a somewhat awkward dance around closing military installations the Pentagon deem unnecessary. In government-speak, it is known as Base Realignment and Closure (BRAC). And since 1988, Congress has closed 97 military bases. It has not been easy. All communities suffered economically. But the hardest decisions have yet to be made, as the Pentagon wants to close many dozens more. And while not insensitive to local economic impact, the Pentagon presents a persuasive argument, citing our smaller military and "force protection" as primary motivations.

Where you stand on BRAC depends almost entirely on where you live. But the fact remains we have all these empty bases, many self-contained mini cities. And they are spread out across the country, just like those at risk in our addict population. Putting the two together would not be difficult. So let's run some numbers. Estimates suggest there are over six million cocaine addicts and a half a million heroin addicts. And the FBI reports the number of larceny-theft offenses in 2002 at around 7 million, costing victims four point nine billion dollars. According to the FBI, these larceny-thefts are largely the work of drug addicts, constituting 59.4% of the overall Crime Index and 67.5% of total property crime. Big numbers all.

The number we most need to determine is how many addicts are responsible. Let's start with 10%. That would mean 650,000 drug addicts commit 7,000,000 crimes, or about 11 each per year, less than one a month. I don't think so. Ask any cop and you'll hear that addicts are trying to steal something almost every day, and hit more often than not, suggesting 10% may be on the high side. So let's look at 5%, or 325,000 addicts. Each would be committing around 2 crimes a month, still below what makes sense. So what does?

Let's look at it a different way. You're a crack addict. You may not smoke it every day but binge when you do, spending several hundred dollars trying to get well. Say you do that four or five times a month. You need $800, maybe a grand. With no visible means of support, you must steal and fence nearly $3000 in TVs and DVDs and whatnot for the money. That's about $40,000 per annum.

So how many $40,000 a year crack addicts does it take to steal four point nine billion dollars worth of personal property? Around 115,000, if you include another 10,000 heroin addicts equally so engaged. That 125,000 grand total represents less than 2% of the entire addict population and a fair estimate of those most in need of asylum. Yet there will be those who balk at paying the freight.

So don't. Let those cocaine addicts living productive lives, as well as all our casual users, do most of the heavy lifting. You can live with that, right? If we have around six million functioning addicts, then we probably have twice that in casual users, or roughly eighteen million total. Legalization will create few new cocaine addicts, but likely add to the casual use number, inching the total closer to twenty million. If each averages 2 grams per month, a reasonable guess, total yearly consumption for all will be roughly four hundred and eighty million grams. But remember, we're talking about *grams* here. And there are 28 in every ounce.

An ounce of pure cocaine can be made for $20. And with virtually no R&D costs, or any need for consumer testing, pharmaceutical companies can make a 50% gross profit selling ounces wholesale to drugstore chains for $30. Who in turn sell it over the counter for $10 a gram, grossing $280 per ounce, but allowed only the same profit margin as Big Pharma. When you do the math and give everyone their cut, you'll find close to three billion dollars on the table, net. But that is still about two billion shy. Don't worry. Be comforted all of us doing drugs recreationally will fully fund those otherwise committed. We'll gladly pay all the freight. Only this time we will demand a far better bang for our buck.

Which brings us back to those 97 decommissioned military bases. Government could lease to private concerns those installations geographically situated and best suited for conversion to drug asylums. Base housing capacity would determine the number of residents, with staffing levels and medical facilities sufficient to properly care for all. The emphasis will be on helping addicts get well, without passing judgment on those unable. It will not be idyllic, but it will be safe. Inside *and* outside. And considering the certainty several dozen more bases on the BRAC list will close, a good chance remains there will be excess capacity, limiting the number of bases chosen.

So I would expect communities with closed bases to actively lobby for that opportunity. I would also expect them to have stiff competition. To support this notion, all we need do is look at the aggressive manner in which many communities lobby to have prisons built in their backyard. Prisons, it must be noted, being constructed to house the projected number of individuals we expect to convict for drug-law violations. It would seem to be one of those "six of one or half a dozen of another" situations. And given the choice, many communities might just prefer non-violent drug addicts to hardcore criminals. Because with legalization, it will only be the hardcore criminals sent to your backyard.

So, yes, expect stiff competition. But a cloistered drug asylum will not have the same economic impact on communities, though any rain in a drought is good. However, when compared to prisons they perform just as well, arguably better. Prisoners do not get to go to town with visiting family, buying clothes and eating burgers and in a hurry to get back. Drug asylum residents, those wanting to go to town, would be almost invisible and harmless. An escaped criminal, on the other hand, would not. The only losers in this competition are companies that build penitentiaries, but what American in their right mind believes prison construction should be a growth industry?

The premise for drug asylums is not "out of sight, out of mind." Actually, it is quite the opposite. We will know exactly where they are, and when we drive by in our cars and SUVs, many of us will be mindful of a prayer, the most frequent being "There but for the grace of God go I." Our children will know drug asylums are for the sick, generating their compassion instead of condemnation, all the while providing a cautionary tale for life. (Add drug asylums to the list of elementary school field trips and expect wiser lifestyle choices later on.) And the inevitable few who become future residents will have a better chance of getting well when told they are sick, not criminal.

Reaching out to assist our addicts at risk can be best accomplished by social service programs, the medical community and, whenever possible, families. It defies logic to believe these addicts will prefer a life of crime and constant danger to one of sanctuary with free drugs, though we should expect many will be reticent to come forward, fearing it all too good to be true. But no addict will sit on that fence for long, and virtually all will come down on the asylum side. Another fair expectation is that many will never leave. Yet it is quite possible, given a change of scenery and a renewed sense of hope, there will be those who can reclaim their place as productive members of society.

Society must also come to grips with those already behind bars. Anyone in our penal system for simple drug possession, with no priors for anything more serious, should be quickly released. There could be an orderly process for pardon, one no less expedient as Gerald Ford used for Richard Nixon. After all, if we can forgive Nixon, we can surely forgive all those unfairly affected by his drug war. But in our litigious society there will be demands for some sort of reparation.

We should resist. Freedom will be its own reward, but only if corporate America sees value in those freed. These individuals will want jobs, and deserve a fair shake. And while it may be wishful thinking to hope those pardoned would seek employment in drug asylums, sometimes opportunity has a funny knock.

And then there is all that marijuana business. My guess is about 30 or 40 million of us smoke it, some more frequently than others. And most marijuana America smokes is commercial-grade and imported. We get it from Mexico and South America and, to a lesser degree, Jamaica. The buzz is nice, not great, but still sells for as much as one hundred seventy-five dollars an ounce. The rest of what we smoke is homegrown and of decidedly higher quality. I readily admit to a preference for this variety, but it makes me crazy an ounce of it costs more than an ounce of gold. Legalization will make the whole business a homegrown home run, even as pot prices drop like a stone.

But who gets to sell it and where will you buy it? As much as Amsterdam has the right idea on cannabis use, their sales and marketing model may not be our ideal. Little coffee shops where you can buy and smoke marijuana and hashish are not so few and far between, and even some restaurants, like the upscale *Grasshopper*, where they sell red Lebanese hash next to red velvet cake, don't mind a puff or two between courses. This model works well because Amsterdam lends itself to getting around on foot and seems more friendly to bicycles than cars, with public trams the most popular mode. Americans drive everywhere and can't smoke anywhere, so that's not going to work.

What will work is what works now. Our marijuana trade is akin to the pizza business, you either pick-up or get delivered. It is simple and efficient and has stood the test of time. I call my friendly marijuana merchant and listen to the menu, then place my order. And I like delivery. But there are times when you can't always get what you want and must wait a spell – vagaries of the marijuana business legalization will eliminate. Gone also will be the need to import commercial-grade pot, as our farmers can grow it here just as good and probably better. Persnickety horti-culturalists will concentrate on the connoisseurs among us, offering as many tasty treats as Ben & Jerry's. And a cadre of marijuana merchants, just a phone call away, will broker it all.

So, how much money is in marijuana? A lot. Whether we like it or not, legalization will likely increase the number of smokers. For the sake of argument, let's say there will be fifty million. And assume each smokes just one ounce every three months, putting the annual total at approximately two hundred million ounces. Growing marijuana is cheap and easy and could sell wholesale at $2.50 per gram, or $70 an ounce. That comes to fourteen billion dollars. At an average retail price of $5 per gram, which is similar to the price in Amsterdam, America will spend twenty-eight billion dollars on marijuana. Taxing the whole shooting match at 10% will generate yearly revenues of nearly four billion dollars, covering cocaine's shortfall in asylum funding, with another two billion left over.

But will we be able to collect it all? Probably. We can expect our farmers to play by the rules, reporting honestly the amount of marijuana they sell, and not be surprised they are happy paying the 10% tax. But the bulk of the tax burden will fall to our sellers. So who keeps them honest, who will help ensure they play by the rules? Well, I propose we enlist all those happy farmers and persnickety horticulturists. And just for the grin it gives I suggest we resurrect the Marijuana Tax Act. For a nominal annual fee, say $50, even $100, sellers are issued something like a credit card that all growers would swipe through a reader, verifying and validating the transaction. Simple.

And collecting the rest shouldn't be much more difficult. We allow sellers access to the classifieds, maybe nothing more than a catchy name, phone number and their Marijuana Tax ID number, and cheaters will rarely prosper. And bet most marijuana merchants will pay the tax, all vying to be that first legit marijuana millionaire. All the ones I know sure support such an idea. Already being in the trade is seen as a nice advantage, allowing them to profit most in a market that will normalize in short order, just like the pizza business. And any marijuana black market will be small, as there will be literally no financial incentive for smokers to buy from it. I know I won't. Will you?

At what age should you be allowed to legally buy marijuana? Should it be 21, the same benchmark we set for alcohol? Or make it too easy at 18, like we do now with tobacco? No, on both counts. I believe an appropriate age would be 20. Why? Simply put, stoners pose fewer dangers to society than drunks. Many in our law enforcement ranks and most medical professionals agree on this point, even if they oppose both. I would even argue access to cannabis a year before alcohol will lead to less drinking later on, citing our appreciation for moderation as my main thrust. Because for most of us so inclined, altering the rigors of reality requires only a soft touch of intoxication.

To further bolster this argument, I need only reference two times in American history, those surrounding the passage of the Harrison Narcotics Act of 1914 and the immediate aftermath of Prohibition repeal in 1933. Before Harrison, most opiate habitués gravitated toward less potent derivatives and were satisfied. After Harrison, those drugs all but disappeared as the emerging black market focused almost exclusively on heroin, denying us our natural inclination toward moderation and obviating any application of the responsible use theory. With the repeal of Prohibition, hard liquor lost its grip and beer regained its position as America's drink of choice, as many preferred the more moderate effect. And since marijuana provides the softest touch of all, expect repeal to make it the poster child of moderation and our best example of responsible use.

Just one question remains. Will we screw it all up? Maybe. But only if we allow the government to do anything more than collect revenue and regulate. They will keep the game's score, and for the very first time have per capita data reflecting hard numbers, replacing all their crystal ball calculations. They should discourage any advertising by pharmacists and support price-fixing, keeping the business profitable but boring, and be ready to regulate if anyone gets excited. Yet they must allow the free-market system to supply whatever demand develops and then trust us our common sense, something we maintained during our peace with drugs and throughout the war. So there is no reason to believe it will suddenly fail us when repeal restores the peace. Not a one.

Well, there you have it. That's my take on how we play the game. Am I right or wrong? Probably. But however off in either direction, I don't expect it to be by very much. I'm not reinventing the wheel here, you know, and it's not exactly rocket science. Much is simply common sense, based on the belief we all share that same indomitable desire to do the right thing and are guided by much the same conscience, defining us as a nation. The rest is less visceral but equally definitive: we just love to play games. And if there is anything we love more than playing games, it's winning them. We can win this game too, but that really isn't the best part. Wait until you see our trophy.

It will be nothing short of stunning. How else to describe an American landscape so suddenly transformed by such a massive and unprecedented drop in crime? Even if the FBI report is off by as much as 15%, America will still experience an across the board reduction greater than 50%. The rate and profile of crime will resemble that last seen in the 50s. It won't be *Happy Days,* but it will be close. And for a moment we just might not know what to do with ourselves, spellbound by the magic wand effect. It is certainly worth thinking about. Which is all that I am asking you to do.

Breathe deeply America.